# FIRST AID IN BEREAVEMENT

John N Greenwood

*By the same author*
Tickets to Heaven

Copyright © 2020 by John N Greenwood

All rights reserved. No part of this book may be reproduced or transmitted in any form or by any means, electronic or mechanical, including photocopying, recording, or by any information storage and retrieval system – except in the case of brief quotations embodied in critical articles or reviews – without permission in writing from its publisher,

The scripture quotations contained herein are from the New Revised Standard Version Bible, Anglicized Edition, copyright©1989, 1995 National Council of Churches of Christ in the USA. Used by permission. All rights reserved.

# Contents

PREFACE ..................................................................... 5
INTRODUCTION ........................................................ 7

PART 1 WHAT TO EXPECT ...................................... 11
1 DEATH AND GRIEF ARE NORMAL EVENTS ............... 13
2 NORMAL EVERYDAY LOSSES ................................... 21
3 MEMORIES .................................................................. 24
4 THE DAY OF BEREAVEMENT ..................................... 30
5 EMOTIONS AND BEREAVEMENT .............................. 36
6 NORMAL EVERY DAY EMOTIONS .............................. 61
7 THE FIRST YEAR AND BEYOND ................................ 65
8 MILESTONES ON THE JOURNEY THROUGH GRIEF 78
9 NORMAL CHANGES TO EXPECT ............................... 82
10 NORMAL SIGNS THAT A PERSON IS COPING WITH THEIR GRIEF ............................................................. 91
11 SIGNS THAT A PERSON IS STRUGGLING TO COPE WITH THEIR GRIEF .................................................. 94

PART 2 WHAT TO DO ............................................... 99
12 WHAT TO DO ABOUT GRIEF .................................. 101
13 WHAT TO DO ABOUT ANNIVERSARIES ................ 107
14 WHAT TO DO ABOUT HELPING SOMEONE ON THEIR JOURNEY THROUGH GRIEF ......................... 117
15 WHAT TO DO ABOUT A NEW RELATIONSHIP ....... 139
16 WHAT TO DO ABOUT MEMORIALS ....................... 155

17 WHAT TO DO WHEN SOMEONE DIES ....................... 159

18 WHAT TO DO ABOUT PROFESSIONAL HELP.......... 160

PART 3 WHAT TO BELIEVE ...................................................... 163

19 THE MESSAGE OF JESUS .................................................... 165

20 THE CHRISTIAN FAITH AND ETERNAL LIFE ......... 186

21 THE CHRISTIAN FAITH AND DEATH ........................ 208

22 THE CHRISTIAN FAITH AND HEALING ................... 215

23 THE CHRISTIAN FAITH AND GRIEF'S BURDEN OF WORRIES ........................................................................................ 226

24 THE CHRISTIAN FAITH AND THE EMOTIONS OF BEREAVEMENT ........................................................................ 232

25 CONCLUSION ........................................................................ 250

# PREFACE

**An easy to follow guide to grief and related issues.**

This book has been written because people are unprepared for grief. They have no means of knowing what the future holds. This route map through grief solves this problem. It provides the reassurance to mourners that they are journeying on a well-trod, well-mapped route. Though not one on which they would choose to be travelling.

For those who see death as the end of all existence, this book can still be of benefit. It provides a route map through grief, and life's worst stresses and strains come when we are on an unfamiliar path in unknown territory.

Many people seeking to come to terms with the loss of a loved one are hindered because they become lost in the unaccustomed emotional changes which occur as a result of the loss. It happens because they have no means of helping themselves to discover where they are on their journey through grief. Or, where that journey might take them next. This book has been written to provide this help.

As a nation, we are unprepared for death. We live as if no one is going to die. Yet the evidence shows that death is inevitable. I have written this book to set death in its true context as a natural part of life. Many books on this subject treat death as if it is something which should not be happening. Death does happen.

I have found that people are unprepared for the death of a loved one, even when death has been long expected. Bereavement leaves people wondering what might happen to me next? Is what I feel customary and to be expected or is it abnormal? Christians question what is happening to them because what the church teaches does not prepare them for the emotional outflow following the death of a loved one? This book answers these questions and meets these issues. It provides an easy to use guide for the journey through grief following the loss of a loved one.Reading this book will help people to see that there is a light at the end of the tunnel of grief and that they are moving towards it.It is a practical guide, not a solution to the difficulties and problems which a few, unfortunately, will encounter. This book, which was seven years in the writing, is not an expert book on bereavement counselling or bereavement therapy and should not be treated as such. For these situations, specialist help should be sort through a professional bereavement counselling service. Where the death is unexpected or is tragic or traumatic, then professional advice may be necessary from the very outset. It can be sought through a doctor or bereavement counsellor.

The purpose of this book is to help the reader to recognise landmarks which will guide them. They reveal that a person is moving in the right direction to emerge from the dark cloud which grief can be. The commonplace experiences of grief following the death of a loved one are described. It informs the person who is in mourning that their feelings are normal. Signalling that it is safe to discuss them with other people because this also is what they too will have felt through their mourning. The more painful experiences of grief are explained. Suggestions are made on how to alleviate the emotions associated with grief. Mourners are helped to progress in their new life without the physical presence of their loved one. The closing chapters set out the practical help which the Christian faith can be in the journey through grief.

# INTRODUCTION

**The book you need to read before you need to read it.**

Everyone is going to suffer a bereavement. This book will help you to reduce the emotional impact of the resulting grief. 80% to 90% of people find their way through such a loss with the help of friends and relatives. This book is for you. It will arm you with what to expect—thus avoiding surprises. It will support you with suggestions on how to prevent the worst excesses of grief. The last section will highlight the help to be gained from the teaching of Jesus.

It is a book to be used as a self-help book to assist people in building a new life following the death of a loved one. A new life in which they can once again enjoy friendships, new and old, and blossom and flourish in longstanding and fresh activities. While also remembering with happiness, nostalgia and thankfulness the times shared with their lost loved one. All of which is what their loved one would want for them. But this will all take time. How long will vary from individual to individual, as explained in the book.

In the course of an average lifetime of three score years and ten plus, bereavement will be experienced several times by everyone. Accordingly, this book is a book which you need to read before you need to read it to be prepared for these events which, like it or not, are going to happen to you.

The title First Aid in Bereavement has been chosen because on the journey through grief; there are several parallels with physical illness. The typical common illnesses and injuries such as bumps and bruises and headaches and tummy upsets can be dealt with by oneself, through medical first aid with the help of family and friends. In more severe illnesses, full-blown medical assistance, such as seeing a doctor or a consultant, may be required. A similar situation occurs in bereavement where there are situations when we can also help ourselves, through making use of First Aid in Bereavement supported by family and friends. In more severe cases of grief affecting 10% to 20% of people, the help of a doctor or a counsellor will be required. The book indicates when this may be necessary.

Like any first aid book, it is a self-help book. As such, some people will find some parts of it more helpful than others. In this context, some may wish only to read those sections which they feel will be of most help to them. A statement in bold at the beginning of each chapter explains the nature of the self-help, tendered as first aid, which that chapter offers. It is done to help readers, who choose to, to turn to just the section which they feel will meet their particular need.

This book is an examination of bereavement as a normal and to be expected event in life. It contains suggestions for self-help for the emotional injuries which can arise as a result of bereavement. Should a person's grieving give rise to any concerns which first aid cannot alleviate. Then, as in medical first aid, professional help should be sought immediately. This help can be obtained from a doctor or a bereavement counsellor as advised in the chapter on 'What to do about Professional Help.'

Bereavement is a tragic and traumatic time in everyone's life. On such occasions, a mourner is plunged into an ocean of grief. This book helps to set a course to navigate this ocean of grief. It enables life's journey to be continued without the physical presence of the lost loved one, but with their memory and influence to guide and encourage.

# PART 1 WHAT TO EXPECT

# 1 DEATH AND GRIEF ARE NORMAL EVENTS

**Relief, reassurance and comfort can be obtained through the realisation and acceptance, that the death of a loved one. Followed by the subsequent journey through grief. Are natural and to be expected as part of everyone's life. Though not something which we would readily choose to experience.**

It is normal and natural to feel overwhelmed by a variety of different feelings when told of the death of a loved one. It is what grief is. Usually, on experiencing a second or subsequent death, these feelings are less intense. The experience gained from living through bereavement once enables us to learn what to expect and how to manage our emotions better. It is helpful to accept that death and grief are a normal part of life. By doing this, we open the door to talking about them before we first encounter them. It helps us to cope with them when they first occur in our lives or at any subsequent time.

That death is a normal part of life can be seen from the fact that all will die. That grief is a normal and natural part of life can be seen from the statistic that all grieve when someone they love dies.Death is a normal part of life. We should expect it and prepare for it as we do for a holiday or a marriage or other major event in our lives. Our genetic make-up derived through evolution has death inbuilt into it. We are genetically programmed to die, so we should not be surprised when a death occurs. Grief is a normal part of life. Grief is the natural way in which we all respond to the death of a loved one. It is through the process of grieving that our minds and bodies undertake the process of healing themselves. We should expect an extended period of grief to be our response when someone very close to us dies.

When we are ill and visit the doctor, it is a relief to be told that our illness is a well-known illness from which anyone may suffer and then recover. It can also be a relief to realise that our grief is the expected response to the death of a loved one, from which everyone will suffer and will then recover. As with a severe illness, it is a time in our lives which no one wishes to experience. In the case of recovery from a severe illness, healing will take some time and will leave some after effects, which may remain with us for the rest of our lives. In the case of grief, recovery will take some time and will leave some after effects, which will remain with us for the rest of our lives.

Much of the emotional uncertainty surrounding our journey through grief arises because society as a whole does not regard bereavement as a normal and natural occurrence in everyone's lifetime. Death is such a taboo subject in our 21st-century society, that grief following a death is seen as something unnatural and therefore, something alien which "should not be happening." Rather than accepting it as the normal and the natural reaction following the death of someone we love. When we receive a cut, then we expect to bleed. When a loved one dies, we have in effect been cut emotionally, and our grieving can be seen as our natural response of emotional bleeding. Just as the natural bleeding from a cut is the normal means for its healing, so also is grief the universal means for the natural healing of our emotional wound.

All experience the impact of another's death, whether that person is close to us or someone we do not know. We all have experiences of death and the ensuing emotions of grief. There are those experiences which are personal, and we experience at first hand arising from the death of close friends and relatives. We encounter death at second hand through talking to people, who convey their own experiences of these events. We have understandings of death which arise from the death of people we do not know which are announced on the news.

In earlier centuries, death came to be accepted much more readily as a part of life when lives were expected to be shorter. In those days, transmittable diseases were much more frequent and unintended deaths more numerous than is the case today. The origin of the Guernsey fisherman's jumpers is an example of a time when death was accepted as a normal part of life. The fishermen's Guernsey jumpers knitted by their wives and mothers from the 18th century onwards contained different patterns each peculiar to the individual fishing villages and communities along Britain's coastline. They also displayed the initials of the fisherman. With no detailed weather forecasts, disaster could overtake the fishing boats at any time with bodies being washed up on a distant shore at a future date. In such circumstances, the fisherman's jumper enabled the body to be identified and returned to the grieving family and community for burial and closure. This destiny and purpose of the jumper would be in the minds of those knitting jumpers for their loved ones. A soldier's "dog tags" serve a similar purpose.

As a result of modern-day society hiding death away, we have come to see death as abnormal. We no longer see death as the inevitable and normal ending of everyone's life. Should the proverbial visitors from Mars come to view our society, then we could forgive them for their first, but the wrong, impression that only 5% of our society die and the rest of us will be left untouched by death. So successful are we in hiding away death.

Death and its impact on those who mourn are mostly swept under the carpet. The exception can be in the case

First Aid in Bereavement

of a celebrity when the media swing into action. It results in the mass media exposure of the funeral rites, and documentaries on the life of the deceased. However, little or nothing is offered by the media to support those who grieve. Either practically or spiritually or emotionally.

In the normal course of a lifetime, almost everyone is destined to grieve for the loss of their two parents, and 50% can expect to grieve for the loss of a spouse or partner. Yes, death will inevitably visit us very closely at least two or three times in an average lifetime. To this, we can add the deaths of four grandparents (two for each of our parents) plus uncles and aunties, and friends. Some of these deaths may be as equally close to us as the death of a partner or parent. Death is not such an infrequent visitor after all. Everyone will die. Everyone will experience grief when it follows the death of someone close to them. However, in our 21st-century society, there are no widely accepted social customs which help us to grieve for the death of a loved one. Either in the popular media or society as a whole.

The Victorians, like the ancient Egyptians, had death and grief carefully regulated. Today, in an age stressing individualism, we may not approve of their collective requirements on how everyone should grieve. The Victorians, however, did face up to the reality that death was normal and inevitable. They took practical measures to help people to cope with the death of a loved one. Their cemeteries contained ornate stones and monuments. They were visible to all and a reminder to all of the inevitability of death. The living were left in no doubt that they too will pass this way. Crematoria have rendered the need for such reminders of death unnecessary. In response to the funeral service prayer of ashes to ashes, crematoria turn our 80kg bodies into 1kg to 2kg of much more easily disposed of ashes. So today we scatter ashes in some secluded spot where no one, but the bereaved, knows and where no one sees or is reminded of the mortal remains of someone lying here.

On the other hand, today, golf courses and other places are seeing a rise in memorial benches and other artefacts. Do these now serve the same purpose, and meet the same need, as those ornate Victorian tombstones? Is this, another example of a return to Victorian values, back to basics under another guise?

The Victorians set a time for mourning and the dress to go with it. It enabled those meeting the bereaved to know, at a glance, without the need to ask or pry, of the sad loss in their lives. Others were thus prepared and knew how to respond to such a meeting. It also gave the bereaved the security of knowing that others would understand their bereavement from their clothing without their need to tell. They also had the security of knowing how to and for how long to mourn. It met the psychological and emotional need for mourning in a socially acceptable manner. Today people are left to grieve as they please. It might suit the more eccentric, but leaves the majority bereft as to what to do or what to expect.

To die is a perfectly normal and natural event in everyone's life. That people grieve, after the death of someone close to them, is a natural and normal event in everyone's life. Grieving is our natural and normal way of healing ourselves. The shock of the death of someone close and the subsequent journey through grief can be likened to undergoing a major operation and the recovery from the trauma of that operation and the subsequent journey through recovery. Following significant surgery, the patient is emotionally and physically in need of recuperation. They recognise the need to take care of oneself to enable this recuperation to happen.

# First Aid in Bereavement

Similarly, there is the need to recognise the need to care for oneself to recuperate from the normal shock of the death of a loved one which will have a similar effect. In recovering from a major operation, people look towards returning to life as they knew it. They are seeking to return to their customary life, as far as is possible and as soon as is possible. Doing the same activities with the same people we know. For these friends and relatives are the people best-placed to support and aid the recovery, both from a major operation and from grief.

The journey through grief is the means of recuperation from the death of a loved one. The aim should be to also look towards returning to life as it was known. At the same time, remembering that this will not be entirely possible, for the loved one is no longer there. With this in mind, the objective should be to keep life as routine as possible. Through doing the same things as have always been done with the same people. By outwardly doing the things that would generally be done then there is inward reassurance that everything is OK and as it should be. A moment of thought reveals that this is not the case, for the death of the loved one has occurred. Such usual and routine activities will keep the mourner in touch with friends and relatives who care, thus enabling them to help and support. These friends and relatives are the people best-placed to support and aid a person on their journey through grief.

In thisnew life without the physical presence of other loved one, the aim will be to continue those parts of the old life which it is wished to do so. While at the same time carrying the memories and influences of the lost loved one. During this time, new interests and new activities will be taken on to be integrated into the new life. Following a significant operation, a cure is looked for, which will enable the usual familiar lifestyle to be resumed. Following the death of someone close to us, there is no such cure, for the life to be returned to is a life without the loved one.

Nevertheless, it is necessary, in like manner to resume the normal life with which the mourner is so familiar as soon as and as entirely as is possible. The effects of a major operation are carried forward. Also, the loss will be carried throughout the survivor's life, albeit with less intensity with the passing of the months and years.

If it is known beforehand what the effects will be of something which is going to happen. Then when that event occurs, the shock of the event and impact of its aftermath are lessened considerably. Should the course which the normal and natural journey through grief will take be known. It enables a person to manage better the shock of losing their loved one. It will lessen the impact of the blow which grief is. Grief comes as a result of the shock of realising that someone has died. The emotions which are called grief are the natural emotions which everyone experiences when they receive such a shock. Grief is the natural and normal way of healing after the shock of bereavement. Just like any shock, the loss leaves people numb and with their emotions working overtime. All as a result of the emotional closeness felt to the person who has died. Thus, the grief, at hearing that 100 people have sadly been killed in an earthquake on the other side of the world, is far less than the pain felt when just one person has died who was known well. In that initial onset of the shock of grief, it is easy to think that what is being experienced is not normal. It is easy for a person to feel that they should not be feeling this way, as in the case of an illness. It leads to people immediately reaching for some cure either from a doctor or counsellor. There is no such cure for grief, as there might be for an illness, with a pill or corrective operation or another form of treatment.

# First Aid in Bereavement

Grief is a type of shock and shocks are perfectly normal in this life. We should, therefore, understand that what is happening to us in grief is normal, and it is the body's and mind's way of dealing with the shock of the death. The journey through grief is one of life's customary journeys difficult and harrowing though it can be. We should approach grief, not with the feeling that this is not normal and should not be happening to me as might be the case with an illness. Instead, we should approach grief with the feeling this is normal and sadly will happen to me and to everyone at some time in their lives. Doctors and counsellors can help. However, grief is to be seen not as unnatural, but as a normal experience. It is something which everyone has to journey through at some time in their one lives. We all will at sometimes in our life have to come to terms with our grief. Grief gives rise to emotions which no one wants to experience. However, grieving is something which everyone will experience at some time in their lives. Grieving is the universal way to recover from the shock of bereavement.

# 2 NORMAL EVERYDAY LOSSES

**Relief, reassurance and comfort can be gained from a deeper understanding of our emotions associated with the loss of a loved one. It can come about when these emotions are compared with similar less intense emotions which occur when we experience other losses in our lives.**

The loss of a loved one has a tremendous impact on our lives. It leaves a hole which can never be filled. Understanding of the emotional impact which follows the death of a loved one can be gained when it is realised that these are the same emotions experienced at other times of loss, albeit at a much lesser intensity.

Grief is the normal and natural response to the loss of a loved one through death. It triggers the same emotions as are experienced with any other form of loss. Life is full of losses. This statement is made not to fill the reader with despair. It is to emphasise that the loss experienced in bereavement is at one end, a very distant painful end, of a spectrum of losses which occur throughout our life. A brief but incomplete summary of these losses includes; the loss of the comfort of the womb on being born; the loss of the continuous security of home on beginning to attend nursery school; the loss of the safety of nursery school on beginning to participate in primary school; the loss of primary school on joining secondary school; the loss of school life on moving on to work or university; the loss of being single on getting married or gaining a partner; the loss of freedom on having children. As we grow older, there are more emotionally demanding losses experienced when close friends and family die. Interspersed amongst these losses are others; the loss of friends and family who have moved away or emigrated; the loss of pets which have died; the loss of relationships through fallings-out; the loss of a job through redundancy; the loss of a spouse, parent or child through a divorce; the loss of a home due to repossession of the house; the loss of prestige or self- esteem. Not to mention less demanding losses including as a child the loss of a toy, the loss of possessions, losing our way, the loss of position in your sport's team (being dropped) and many more. You may wish to list these in the order of the impact they have had on your life. These losses trigger the same feelings and emotions which are experienced in grief though at a much lower level of intensity. Concerning more severe losses, if the stress of the loss of a spouse or partner due to bereavement is rated as 100. Then on the same scale (the equivalent emotional stress or bereavement effect of the loss) in the case of divorce, this would be about 70-80 and loss of job about 50. Other bereavements such as the loss of a parent would be about 60-70. These are estimates which only give a feel for the measure of a loss as each loss is very much influenced by the personalities and experiences of the people involved and the personal background to the loss. To help put things in perspective on a similar scale, we might rate the loss of a bank card or mobile phone at 10 or 15.

In all of these other losses, the emotions felt are the same as, though not as powerful as, the ones felt when we are bereaved. As an example, take the loss of a bank card. The first reaction is one of disbelief and denial. A person may even declare "I do not believe I have lost it. It must be here somewhere." Or "I cannot have lost it. I had it only this morning." As the realisation that it is lost sinks in there is the feeling of shock and numbness. Disorganisation and confusion may be displayed as random searches for it are made in pockets, in shopping bags and about the house. There is a yearning to see it lying in a chair or under the settee. There may be feelings of being overcome by anxiety, panic or even fear at the prospect of the possible consequences of the loss. Anxious questions are asked, such as, "What am I going to do now?"

There may be anger for not taking greater care of what was done with the card. There may even be anger at God for the loss. It may even be exclaimed, "God, where is it?" Or "Oh God, why did I lose it?" Implying that God is in some way at fault. There may be feelings of blame for others. Perhaps the shop assistant at the shop till, whose conversation was a distraction—thus preventing the necessary concentration on where the card was put. There may also be feelings of guilt and regret over the loss as it is reflected that more care should have been taken with what was done with the card. There may be feelings of emptiness and depression as the loss, and the consequences for fraud are fully realised. Other everyday losses trigger these self- same emotions. It is possible to reflect on the feelings following such losses. These are precisely the feelings felt when a loved one is lost. Thus, the feelings associated with loss through being bereaved are not new. Even should this be the first occasion of the death of someone close. However, these emotions will be far more acute in the case of bereavement.

By recalling the successful routes taken through any other such losses, this will be a reassurance that the journey through grief can also be successfully undertaken. This process makes us realise that these emotions and feelings are not entirely new. On past occasions, they have been journeyed through. All be it a far less daunting task. The awareness of these other losses and how they were handled can be a positive influence on how to cope with the loss through death. Bereavement, however, is a final loss, with no possibility of an immediate return to the status quo, as there would be should the bank card be found.

# 3 MEMORIES

**Relief, reassurance and comfort can be gained from the knowledge that our memories of our loved one have parallels with many of the other memories in our life. They are to be treasured. Just like our other memories, there will come a time when they can be recalled with feelings of happiness, nostalgia and gratitude**

Memories of a lost loved one are to be treasured. Even though initially, they may well bring with them feelings of intense sadness and grief. Later, in many cases, much later, they will be treasured with nostalgia, gratitude and happiness. Memories of a lost loved one can trigger such deep feelings of grief and sadness that they can be overwhelming. Help in coping with these feelings can be found. It occurs in realising that these memories, though more intense, are similar to other memories of friends and relatives who can be thought about and who are still alive. These memories can be recalled with feelings of happiness, nostalgia and gratitude. The aim should be to seek to recall the memories of the lost loved one in a similar fashion with happiness, nostalgia and gratitude. However, this will be difficult in the time immediately following the death. It may take many months or years, even a decade or more before this can be done.

The one big difference is that in the case of the lost loved one, there will never be the opportunity again to make more memories with them. There are also some similarities to this with other memories. Such as memories of our children in childhood. This is a situation which cannot be returned to, to make more memories, though the children are still present as adults. Also, memories of school friends with whom contact has been lost. Another example is memories of friends or relatives who have emigrated. As a result, there may be limited or no further opportunities to make more memories with them.

Being reminded of the deceased loved one will produce memories of them, and this, in turn, will trigger grief. These reminders come in many forms. Some memories are unexpectedly triggered by something someone else says, or a place name on the news or a familiar mannerism seen in someone else, which recalls the lost loved one. In some cases, memories are half expected to be triggered, for example, when attending a wedding or a funeral. Some can be triggered by reflecting on old photographs or watching a television programme which used to be viewed together. All of this is not new for these triggers also served to prompt the recall and the sharing of memories with your loved one when they were alive. For example, when planning a holiday when our loved one was alive and well. On such occasions, the opportunity would arise to reflect on memories of past holidays in that place or elsewhere perhaps as old photographs were looked at together. A place name on the news would be a reminder of memories to talk about and share with the loved one when they were alive and well. These memories, recalled together while our loved one was still alive, are the same memories. Then they did not have the poignancy which they have on their recall following the death of our loved one. For, now, our loved one is no longer here to share the memories. One of the long-term aims must be to be able to recall these memories with similar feelings of gratitude, nostalgia and happiness. It was how we felt about these memories before the bereavement when we recalled those memories with our loved one alive and well. The time taken for this to become possible might be as short as a few months or 2 to 5 years or as long as 10 to 15 years or longer. How long this will

# First Aid in Bereavement

take will vary from individual to individual for no two journeys through grief are identical. It is so even when that journey is undertaken by the same person perhaps grieving for one parent and then at a later date for their other parent.

The memories, recalled when grieving, are part of the whole spectrum of memories which are stored in our minds. Throughout life, we interact with other people. This interaction creates memories. Our contact is more significant and most intense with those people who are closest to us. It is with these people that we create the most intense and lasting memories. When someone dies, then it is not possible to make any more memories with them. This inability to make any more memories is found in other phases of life. It occurs when there is a move away from a location, especially when we move to another country. Then our friends are left behind, except for the memories of those friends. Or when we leave school or university and lose touch with once close friends leaving just the memories of them.

Apart from bereavement, the effect of the impact of memories on someone's life is at its most intense form in the case of two people deeply in love but living apart. In this situation some of the emotions associated with bereavement surface, though not with the same intensity. There is a yearning for the absent loved one, perhaps looking at their photograph, to relive the memories of the happy times which were spent together. There are feelings of emptiness and sadness and numbness when apart. There is a feeling of loss when the partner is not physically present. There are times of daydreaming of the lover being once again present. Even imagining their caress and touch in dreams when asleep. In their absence, the partner feels low and may also exhibit some of the symptoms of depression. Though similar, the meaningful difference between these feelings, and the related feelings associated with bereavement, are that it is known that the physical relationship is soon to be restored.

There are feelings, which impact on people in bereavement as they recall memories of their departed loved one. These feelings are part of the same continuum as those feelings, which are faced with many times in life, through the recall of our memories of people we know well. The noteworthy difference is that in grief, these feelings strike with much greater force and lasting impact.

We all have memories of everyone we have ever met. These include the people lived with now and seen on a daily or regular basis. The memories of people met and not seen for several days or weeks or months or even years. The memories of people from our past, who have moved away and we may never meet again. The people now adults and of whom we have childhood memories. The people we have known who are now deceased. These memories form a continuum in their emotional impact on us. The most significant emotional impact coming from our memories of people who had been the closest to us and are now deceased. When someone dies, we can no longer create memories anymore with them, whereas in the case of the living, we can create new memories. It is the fundamental difference between our memories of the living and the dead.

At first glance, the world around us seems a very solid and secure place. As we talk with our relatives, friends and acquaintances, they too seem very solid and stable. We shake hands with them, touch them and interact with them. However, when they have left us and are out of sight, how do we know them? We know them through our memories. These memories are not so reliable and secure. This fact can be seen in that individuals will have different memories of the same event. This will arise because people have interacted with people in different ways and on diverse occasions or seen an event from a different perspective. The precise memories will be different for each individual involved. This brief review reveals that what we know and feel about the people we know when we are no longer with them, is solely based on our memories. Yes, these memories are updated from time to time when we meet people again. Yes, these memories can be updated as a result of modern technology which allows us to communicate with each other. However, we are not in each other's physical presence. In the final analysis, memories are all that we have of one another. Even when we meet with someone, it is our memories, which informs us what to expect of that other person. It is a similar situation when someone dies. In the final analysis, when we are not in their presence, memories are all that we have of dead or living people.

As parents, we reflect from time to time on our memories of bringing up our children. Perhaps we might have recourse to photographs or videos, CDs and DVDs to refresh and remind us of those times and memories. However, there is no way we can go back and make new memories of bringing up our children. Once their childhood has passed away, then we cannot return to knowing our children as children again. We do, however, have our memories. This is a similar situation, to the situation in bereavement, in terms of our memories. The emotional impact of grief is the difference between the two. This emotional impact colours our feelings and our reactions to those memories. Our memories of a deceased person are shrouded in sadness. Our memories of our children in childhood are tinged with nostalgia, gratitude and happiness. The goal of our journey through grief is to come to a time when we can view those memories of our lost loved one in the same way. Also viewing those memories with nostalgia, gratitude and happiness. The time it takes for this to happen maybe a few months, a year or two or in some cases, many years. It will depend on the circumstances and the individual personalities involved.

It is good to have a tangible resource to trigger memories of our loved one from time to time. It can be achieved by displaying a favourite photograph(s), or collage of photographs, of the loved one in a prominent position at home. Also, a photograph album can be specially produced to record their life. (See the chapter What to do about Memorials.) The danger lies in allowing such a collection to become a shrine which controls us and draws us to it. We must remain in control, making a choice when to visit it from time to time. When we do, reflecting on our memories seeking to recall them with nostalgia, gratitude and happiness. The memories of our loved one are in the same continuum or range as the memories of other people who are not present with us.

## 4 THE DAY OF BEREAVEMENT

**Relief from the anxiety of what lies ahead in the journey through grief can be found, by comparing that journey through grief to the ordered pattern of the phases of a day. The periods of the day inevitably follow in their ordered fashion. The darkest hours of the night passing into dawn and then on into the sunlight of the daytime. In like manner, the phases of the journey through grief will also inevitably follow a similar ordered pattern, from the darkness to the light.**

That grief will be experienced following the loss of a loved one is perfectly normal and natural. Everyone feels this way. There will be individual variations, and on the journey through grief, feelings and attitudes will change over time. These changes can be likened to another natural occurrence. It is the passage of a day. During the journey through grief, it is helpful to compare the changing stages on that journey with the changing phases of a day. Always remembering, that just as the periods of a day will follow a prescribed pattern so also will the stages of our journey through grief. The passage of each day follows the same natural pattern, though the length of time for each stage of grief will be much, much longer than the minutes or hours of the phases of a passing day. The stages of grief can be compared to the following periods in the passage of day;

the sun setting,
the evening falling,
the dark of the night time,
the breaking light of the dawn,
the sunrise
and finally the brightness and sunshine of a new day.

The journey through grief follows a similar regular pattern but lasting for far longer than a day. Just as we can be sure that each natural and scheduled part of the day will give way to the next, so also in grief will one stage naturally and routinely give way to the next.

The moment of death can be likened to the sun setting and the immediate period after that is the fall of the evening. The fall of the evening is a reminder of other falls associated with death. The falling autumn leaves and those who fall in battles. This time of grief is marked by feelings of denial and disbelief, and of shock and numbness before the full impact of grief overtakes us.

Then follows the darkness of the night when the fullness of our grief is upon us. Darkness engulfs the mourner, and they feel alone and lost in surroundings which are familiar but somehow different and hard to make out and understand. This darkness arises from the loss of the companionship of our loved one, who in the past, had illuminated the way. Now familiar things may worry or confuse and there is a struggle to perceive and make sense of what is going on around us. Just as someone might struggle to make out what is the layout of a familiar but darkened room which seems unfamiliar when seen in gloom and darkness. Feelings of disorganisation and confusion characterise this time. These feelings can be likened to the experience of trying to cross a darkened well-known room when the lights are out.

There may be feelings of anxiety, panic and even fear, such as might be felt walking alone down a familiar road on a night with the street lights out. There may be a lashing out at the darkness through emotional outbursts of anger, resentment, blame, rage, hate and even terror. Reflecting on the darkened surroundings consciences may be plagued by feelings of guilt and regret. These feelings may result in sleepless nights, contributing to increasing feelings of overall listlessness and lack of energy. This night time of bereavement may last a few weeks or a few months, for some people a few years or even longer. These emotions will be less intense for some people than for others. This night time will not be without its false dawns, which are to be welcomed for they are the herald of the sunrise, which lies ahead. Then, perhaps when the night is at its deepest, signs of the dawn can be seen creeping into your life, in the same manner, that the night sky begins to lighten before the coming sun. Then the light of new hope begins to lighten your life. Just as the world becomes flooded with light as the sun first peeps above the horizon. So comes the rising sun in your life, perhaps in the form of a new relationship, or new friendships or new interests and these, like the sun's rays, begin to burn away the darkness. The warm, bright sunshine of a new day comes. The embracing of a new life without the physical presence of our loved one can be compared to welcoming the rays of the newly risen sun.

The risen sun reveals the roads and pathways which previously were shrouded in the darkness of the night. This new dawn enables a path through life to be seen laid out into the future. It will of necessity, be a new route chosen by the mourner for the loved one is no longer there as a guide and travelling companion. Along this new pathway, the halting steps of a new life without the loved one can be made. The darkness of grief is no longer able to shroud thoughts and blight thinking. New plans can begin to be laid for the direction which thenew life will take.

It is possible to now emerge into the full light of day and to continue the building of that new life without the loved one. There is now no darkness to obscure the path which needs to be followed. It will be the path which will lead to the mourner's sunset and death. At this stage of their lives, they may be reluctant to admit to this or even wish to contemplate or acknowledge it. In reality, everyone is journeying to their death.

As the mourner steps out into the light of the day, it does not mean that the darkness lies forever behind them. Just as dark clouds can suddenly appear and blot out the sun in the daytime so also can grief unexpectedly come to ambush us. By now, it has been learnt how to manage grief so that it is no longer overpowering and all-embracing. It has been discovered how to enable grief soon to pass and for life to return to normal. As clouds pass over the face of the sun, so also will the periods of grief pass on. It has been learnt how to let grief have its moment then subside away. This day time of grief will remain for the rest of a person's life, for grief will be carried, albeit a much more comfortable and lighter burden, to the end of this earthly life, to its sunset.

As the mourner moves off into the sunshine of the daytime, old activities are being undertaken, appreciated and enjoyed. New activities and new interests have joined them. The old memories of the old times are now joined by fresh memories of the new day and the new times. Now the mourner is successfully living a new life without the physical presence of their loved one but with their memory and their legacy always with them. The night time of grieving is passed. The memories of the loved one are now a support, an encouragement, a comfort and a source of thankfulness, and perhaps surprisingly a source of nostalgic happiness as the loved one would want them to be. For now, the mourner is in the day time of their loss. They can now look back on the memories of their loved one, with nostalgia, gratitude and happiness; as they pass through the morning and move into the afternoon of their grief in their new life. If not now, in time, they will look at these memories with gladness and happiness, for the night time of grieving is passed when memories brought mainly sorrow and sadness. They now know that they will be able to carry these nostalgic and wonderful memories with them for the rest of their life.

Of course, the timespan we are looking at is much more than a day. For some the night of grieving, may last six months or one or two years. For others up to five years or a decade or more, before the first glimmers of the dawn begin to break. Each of these phases of mourning will have their own pace and length varying from individual to individual. The length of these time frames will be dependent on the personality of the mourner, the nature and closeness of the relationship with the deceased as well as the circumstances surrounding the death. The light of day is the longest. The day time will run to the end of life, and like a typical English day, with its rain showers, there will be the odd shower of tears as grief returns, to be quickly followed by the sunshine of the new life.

Similarly, during the night time of grief, there will be pleasant times when life feels almost normal again before being plunged back into sorrow. In much the same way that pleasant dreams can punctuate sleep in the darkness of the night. The evening will be the shortest as the initial full impact of the shock of loss is experienced. The times of the day are natural and normal, and everyone has to journey through them. Then so also are the times of grief, natural and normal, and everyone has to travel through them at some time in their life. The consolation comes from knowing that just as the day will unfold in its predicted manner, so also, we know that one phase of grief will also take over from the preceding one in a predictable way. It is preferred that this journey take place when grown-up adult children grieve for elderly parents who have lived a long and fulfilled life. But there is no control of this and death can come in the most tragic of circumstances. Whenever the journey through grief takes place, then it will be made up of these set phases which will naturally and normally follow one another just as do the times of the day in their natural and regular order. The night time of grieving and sadness will be followed by the day time of gratitude and happiness for the life of the loved one and all that they meant.

# 5 EMOTIONS AND BEREAVEMENT

**On the death of a loved one, the impact of the emotions, which rise to the fore can overwhelm us. Their effect is reduced by knowing what these emotions will be, and by understanding that they are normal emotions which will play themselves out.**

The truth of the statement set out in bold print above is revealed by the fact that for the majority of people, their emotional experiences following the first death of a parent are much more profound than those experienced following the later death of the surviving parent. It is primarily because having experienced the first death that person is now mindful of the nature of the emotions to be experienced. They are aware that they are normal and to be expected and that they will play themselves out. It is not always the case, for example, if the relationship to the second parent to die was far deeper than that to the first parent to die.

A professional sporting team will find out all they can about their opponents, before a match. It is done to counter and blunt their effectiveness. Similarly, we can also counter the effects which grief can have upon us, by finding out beforehand what the effects will be. With this in mind, we shall examine these emotions. In so doing, we are preparing ourselves for the time when we too will experience those emotions.

The emotions which the loss of a loved one releases are well documented. Knowing that the emotional upheaval which bereavement brings is natural and to be expected is a reassurance. Though it may be difficult to appreciate this when beset by such emotions, also, knowing what these emotions will be is the best way of preparing for them. With these thoughts in mind, the following is an outline of the feelings we can expect to experience as a result of being bereaved.

People who are on their journey through grief more often than not think with their emotions rather than with logic. We must remember this as we come now to review the feelings which are associated with the grief which accompanies being bereaved. We will look at the emotions which we can expect to feel when we are bereaved. These will vary in intensity depending upon the closeness and the nature of the relationship with the deceased person. The strength of these emotions will also be dependent upon the circumstances surrounding the death. Most notably, whether it was sudden unexpected death from illness or following an extended illness, or it was a result of an accident. Some people may not experience some emotions. Some people may experience others with much greater intensity and for a much longer duration than others. Some feelings may dominate. Some may come and go. Some may arise in a different order. We must remember that each person's journey through grief will be different, while at the same time having many areas in common. As a general rule, the following emotions can be expected to be felt during the journey through grief, in the order set out here.

Acknowledgement that these intense emotions will be released is to be found in the following sound advice. The news of a death is to be broken as gently and as sensitively as possible to the recently bereaved. The heightened emotional state of affairs, which will result is also acknowledged by the need for a bereaved person to be handled gently and with much forethought in those first few days of grief.

On hearing of the death, the first reaction to be displayed is not accepting that the death has occurred at all through denial or disbelief.

Non-Acceptance of the death through Denial and Disbelief

Denial or disbelief will be felt most keenly when the death has been sudden and unexpected. Non-acceptance that the death has occurred can serve to cushion us from the full emotional impact of grief. Often when the news of the death is received, people declare "I don't believe it." "You're joking, aren't you"? "It's not possible. I was only speaking to him this morning". Or simply the one word "No!" These normal feelings of denial and disbelief for a second or so seemingly give us a breathing space before we fully appreciate the reality of the death. We, in effect, freeze. In this short period of time, our minds can prepare themselves for the impact of the full shock. It is a similar reaction to when we freeze in our car seats at the sudden and unexpected prospect of an impact with another car or object. The immediate feeling of denial or disbelief in a sense buys us the time to mentally brace ourselves for the full effect of the shock which knowledge of the death will bring.

If these feelings of denial last over several hours or longer, then they provide the time for us to adjust to taking in the sad news gradually. In this response to the death, of denial and disbelief, then in effect what is taking place is that the brain knows the facts. Still, the heart does not wish to know hence giving rise to denial and disbelief. This denial and disbelief may persist, thus shielding the heart from the reality of the loss and the ensuing emotional reaction which will follow. It may be a momentary reaction, or it may persist for several hours or days. Should it continue and cause concern then help should be sort through a doctor or counsellor and certainly this should be done if denial or disbelief continue beyond the funeral.

Feeling Stunned by the news as Shock and Numbness come over us

Accompanying or following after those emotions of denial or disbelief comes the feeling of being stunned as numbness and shock embrace us. These emotions occur most strongly and more acutely in the case of a sudden death. Still, they will also be felt when the loss has been expected, for example, after a long illness. The news of the passing can leave us stunned as shock and numbness come over us. It causes us to freeze, to not want to move on or to not want to react to the death in any way. By doing this, we are in effect, denying that the death has occurred. These reactions also serve as a cushion enabling us to stay in the moment before that dreadful news was delivered. This postponement lessens the full impact of the effect of the shock of the death on our minds. Like denial and disbelief, shock and numbness serve to protect us from the full emotional impact of the loss. Through shock and numbness, we are trying to stop our life in its tracks as we are stunned into immobility mentally and sometimes physically. We try to stay as we were before the news of the death was told to us and so in a sense pretend it hasn't happened, or postpone it happening. We hesitate to move on in our life without our loved one. It is like freezing on a doorstep of a house at night time and not wanting to step outside into the dark unknown. So, we seek to remain within the security of familiar things. It may be a minute, an hour, a day, a week or in very extreme cases for some people even longer before we can even begin to embrace the full impact of the reality of the death. As the shock and unresponsiveness wear off, we can start to come to terms with the death. It may be that we may sense the numbness wearing off. The numbness serves a similar function to the painkilling injec-

# First Aid in Bereavement

tion when we have a tooth filled or extracted. The anaesthesia helps to deaden the pain of our loss, but as is the case with our tooth, as the numbness wears off, we become fully aware of the pain of our loss. Some people may be reluctant to leave their home and so stay with things which are familiar and well-known keeping the situation as if nothing has happened.

Should these feelings persist and prevent the mourner from accepting and beginning to come to terms with the death, then help should be sought from a doctor or counsellor.

Disorientation as our thoughts and actions are characterised by Disorganisation and Confusion

Disorientation is a typical response to the news of the death of someone close to us. Our lives have abruptly been changed. We struggle to adapt to the new order which has been forced on our lives. Our life has been turned upside down making us disorientated just as we would feel unsettled and panicky if someone suddenly, took hold of us and physically turned us upside down. These feelings persist as we begin to take on board the sad news of our loss. When these feelings overcome us, it is challenging to stay focused on what we are doing or to complete tasks. We have difficulty or in extreme cases, find it impossible to plan ahead. With the capability of organising ourselves gone, we lose direction. It leads to not remembering where we have put something down or failure to return something to its proper place when we have finished using it. It also leads to forgetting to pay bills or forgetting to do the necessary shopping as well as not being able to plan a holiday or to arrange to see someone. Tasks may be left unfinished, or we may not get organised even to get started. Should disorganisation and confusion persist, then walls may be built up which become barriers to the outside world. In more extreme cases a mourner may become withdrawn refusing to meet or interact with others, perhaps even refusing to leave the house. This withdrawal and a refusal to interact with others come about because the mourner cannot get organised to do so or plan ahead to do so. Should this situation of isolation arise or there are other related concerns. Professional help should be sort through a doctor or counsellor.

Wanting the Loved One Back expressed through Searching and Yearning

The next two reactions may begin almost immediately but are more likely to occur as the days, weeks and months pass by and are more common where there has been a close emotional, and physical link such as in the case of the death of a spouse or a close parent-child link is broken by death.

There is a yearning for the touch and the reassurance of the presence of the loved one who has died. It results in our minds searching for the presence of our loved one. This searching may also include physical searching as we revisit places where we have strong memories of being there with our loved one. The searching within our minds may be so intense that our minds seemingly find our loved one. The result is that our minds react on occasions as if our loved one is present. It may result in our being aware of the presence of the loved one or even feeling their touch or hearing their voice or their footsteps. We may dream about the person. Do not seek for any profound or noteworthy implications in these dreams for it is only our mind searching for the person who has died. If these events and dreams leave us feeling gratified, peaceful and comforted, then look on them as a blessing to be welcomed. If on the other hand our dreams worry us or distress and trouble us then seek help from a doctor or a

# First Aid in Bereavement

counsellor. Some people report feeling sure of catching a fleeting glimpse of the deceased person in a crowd as another person's voice or looks or disposition recalls that of the loved one. Once again, this is the result of our mind responding to the need to search for the person. While at the same time, yearning for their presence. The result is that our minds seemingly find our loved one. Such occurrences can be viewed as typical aspects of grief as so many bereaved people report experiencing them.

Some people meet this need for the presence of their loved one by retaining a portion of their ashes. It may be done in a small suitably designed urn or have a small portion incorporated in a piece of jewellery. Relevant searches on the internet will find companies who provide this service.

We may use up our energy searching for our loved one in our memories, consciously and subconsciously, as we yearn to have them back. All of this saps our strength and energy and may leave us exhausted, particularly at the end of the day. It helps to explain why bereaved people often complain of feeling drained and having no energy.

Distress manifested in Anxiety, Panic and Fear

Feeling distressed as a result of anxiety and even fear about the new future which lies before us after the death of a loved one is perfectly normal and natural. This distress is similar to, though not so intense, as the worry we feel whenever we face a new situation. For some mourners, however, experiencing these powerful new emotions, already described in this chapter, can be distressing. This distress is caused by there unexpectedness and the overwhelming force with which these emotions come. We find ourselves experiencing anxiety, panic and even fear in having to face these powerful emotions which can be overpowering. These feelings have all the more force because now we have been deprived of our loved one as a companion and helper. Who could calm our response to such a new situation. It can result in the following three emotions arising. Anxiety, panic or fear for the future which arise as we worry or become stressed by questions such as; How will things work out as I look to the future without my loved one? How am I going to cope now? Where can I now turn for help?

These feelings can be a significant part of the grieving experiences of some people. The origin of these feelings may lie in different fields which may or may not be connected. One origin lies in the overwhelming force with which our emotions hit us. Feelings of deep sadness and total despair come like the waves of the sea. We can sometimes even anticipate these waves coming. At other times grief can creep up on us and ambush us. We do not know the strength of these waves until they hit us. Some will literally sweep us off our feet and knock us over in an emotional sense. This experience is very new to us. We may feel anxiety, panic or fear because we think we are in some way abnormal. These waves of grief are alien. We do not comprehend them and struggle to control them. As we are swept along or metaphorically knocked over by these waves of grief, we get the impression that we are out of control and we may be completely overwhelmed by a deep sadness. It can cause panic, and we become fearful and anxious at the prospect of these feelings returning again and again. As these feelings are new to us, then we have no or little experiences of dealing with them. It can be a further cause for anxiety, panic and fear because we do not know what we should do or how to control them when they inevitably return. Some people even claim that they feel that they have so little control over the emotions which arise through the grief that they think they are going mad.

Another source of these feelings can be practical. Arising as a direct result of our loved one no longer being there to fulfil the tasks and the role which they have done in our lives. We just don't know what we are going to do from a practical point of view from now on. These feelings might arise from such questions as. Who will now do the cooking and cleaning? This on the death of a wife. Who will manage the finances? This on the death of a husband. If the passing results in changed financial circumstances, this will cause anxiety as to how to make financial ends meet. So, we experience anxiety, panic and even fear as we contemplate our future life without our loved one. This situation leads to questions like; "Who will now fulfil this role?" "Who will do these things for me now?" "Who will help me now?" "How am I going to cope now?" "What am I going to do?" These thoughts arise more predominantly if we were dependent on that person, or the death has plunged us into financial problems. These feelings can occur as we are left without any apparent answers to the practical issues we face in life. These significant issues face us with our loved one no longer there to help and guide. The result can be that we feel anxiety, panic and even fear.

Other questions may spin into our heads depending on the particular circumstances. For example, whether or not we can continue to hold our family together or whether our life can have any purpose without our loved one. The death of a loved one reminds us of our mortality, and this can be a further cause for fear and anxiety about ourselves as we question when or how we might die? Or we begin to reflect on what happens when we die? With the death of one member of the family comes the realisation that someone else may also die. In the case of a grieving child, their worst fear can be that the surviving parent will also die. It can cause further waves of anxiety, panic and fear as thoughts of having to live through all of this pain again pass through the mind. Anxiety, panic and fear can stem from any or all of the above.

These emotions can be magnified as the shock of the death of our loved one has left us feeling low and with little energy to protect ourselves from such feelings. We have not got the oomph to fight back. We have little strength to work out what we might do, let alone the energy to do it. This can lead to further feelings of anxiety and panic as we recognise that we have not got the drive to plan what we must do to help ourselves.

These feelings will be felt to a greater or lesser extent by everyone on their journey through grief. Help must be sought from a doctor or counsellor should these issues cause any significant concerns. This is especially so if practical problems arise which appear to have no easy solution.

Tangible Effects seen in Physical, Emotional or Bodily Changes

The impact of bereavement and our ensuing grief can result in noticeable effects which can be physically seen or felt in our bodies. The word grieve gives us the word grievous, which means bringing about physical suffering as in the crime of GBH (grievous bodily harm). So, we should expect that to grieve will have some impact on our physical bodies.

The most common effects are that grieving saps our energy and so leaves us tired and exhausted. This is further compounded by our sleep pattern being disrupted, resulting in our inability to sleep, either unable to get to sleep or waking up early or both. This is counterproductive. It is not helpful. As we grieve, we need more sleep and rest than usual. This is so that we can recharge our batteries, to refresh ourselves and to build-up our resilience so that we can get on with rebuilding our lives.

In some people who are particularly adversely affected by grief, other physical symptoms may be apparent. These are well documented and include feeling sick, feeling dizzy, getting headaches, indigestion, heart palpitations, plus changes in appetite. Any existing physical symptoms of a current illness may get worse. The stress of grief can also suppress the immune system making illnesses like colds and flu more likely, or making an actual sickness worse. Our eating patterns may change giving rise to comfort eating, or we may skip meals altogether.

Such effects need to be monitored, and appropriate help sought if necessary, from a doctor or counsellor.

Emotional Outbursts of Anger, Resentment, Blame, Rage, Terror

These emotions can all be triggered by grief, in much the same way as other happenings in life can trigger them. Each can be set off by the least little thing, which acts as the last straw. It can be more so in grief when normality has been stripped away and with it our usual self-control. These emotional outbursts can be likened to exploding fireworks which go off unexpectedly in the dark. Such explosions, even when half expected, startle and shock people. If they are too fierce or too often, they can do damage elsewhere and in unexpected places. Their explosive force can adversely affect those around us and in extreme cases, destroy longstanding friendships and alienate relatives. As in other situations in life, these outbursts explode stress and tension away. As such, they can be useful in removing the stress and anxiety arising out of grief, from the individual mourner at a personal level.

On the other hand, these emotional outbursts can increase the stress and tension in friends and family who become wary of such outbursts. People may even avoid social contact should the eruptions become too frequent or be too forceful. This further isolates the one who is mourning and sets them apart, alienating them from those who may best help them. In a worst-case scenario, the result is that the mourner becomes more and more inward-looking. He begins to feel more and more misunderstood, as such outbursts bring isolation if not criticism and condemnation from friends and relatives. For these reasons alone, these outbursts need to be kept under control.

If any of these emotions form part of your grief journey, then you need to express them outwardly by telling someone you trust how you feel and why you feel this way. This allows you to express your feelings and the underlying cause of your behaviour. This outward expression can be useful for it relieves your inner emotional tension as well as letting people know how you feel. So, talk to someone you can trust about how you think if you have these emotions and especially if they are causing you or anyone else concern. In this way, you will defuse them naturally. It also provides the ideal opportunity for your trusted friend to help you to see things in their real perspective. This will help you to take control of these emotions.

On the other hand, the unnatural bottling up of these emotions, so that they are not expressed at all, can lead to other mental health problems later on. If any of these emotions cause you the mourner concern or raises the concern of friends and relatives, then help should be sort through a doctor or counsellor.

These emotions can stem from many origins some examples are as follows.

First Aid in Bereavement

Anger

The anger which we find expressed by a person who has lost a loved one is not unique to the loss of a loved one. In life, when something is lost, then anger is often expressed. This may be in the form of anger at oneself for losing or misplacing an article, for example, our keys or wallet. Or anger at other people for their part, or perceived role, in causing our loss. Thus, the anger found in grief is part of a continuum of anger which can be found in all the aspects of our lives which involve loss.

Anger arising as a result of grief is the emotion which can do the most damage outwardly to our friendships and relationships and inwardly to the individual concerned. Of all the emotions released by bereavement, it is the one emotion which can work the most to the mourner's detriment. Anger can separate, alienate and estrange the mourner from those people who are the most capable of helping them at this sad time in their lives. It is essential that should anger arise, then we manage our anger and do not let it control us.

When considering the anger present in issues relating to grief, we must differentiate between two types of anger. The first anger which arises because of a genuine failure of duty and care by medical staff or other carers which must be reported to the appropriate authorities. Reporting these legitimate concerns is the best way to assuage this anger. The other type of anger is the anger which stems from our emotional need to blame someone. We want to hold responsible someone or something for the tragedy which has overtaken us in the loss of our loved one. It is this second form of anger which we will consider here. This anger may be directed at medical staff and other professional carers, friends and family who cared for the deceased, ourselves or even God and the dead person. Usually, the feelings stemming from this anger will lessen and disappear over time. It occurs as the full circumstances of the reality of our loss become accepted by ourselves, and we realise that the death of our loved one is no one's fault. This anger can well up and subside almost as quickly as it comes, or it can linger over weeks and months and even years.

The anger felt arises in response to what you think is happening to you as a result of the death of your loved one. One of those feelings is that you have been hard done by. The natural reaction in life when we feel hard done by is to respond with anger. When we lose our loved one, this can quickly lead to a feeling of being hard done by. This is revealed as we often respond by feeling, if not saying, "Why has this happened to my loved one?" "Why has this happened to me?" Feeling hard done by can lead us to search for someone to blame and to be angry at. The death of a loved one, be it sudden, or after a prolonged illness, leaves us with plenty of targets for our anger should we wish to take aim at them. Anger can be aimed at almost anything or nothing.

This anger can have many sources and can be directed at anyone involved in the life of the deceased person. It can be targeted at surgeons, doctors, nurses and carers or relatives. It arises when justly or unjustly, it is felt that not enough had been done to save the life of the person who has died. It can even be directed at yourself if you think that in some way, you too have not done enough. We may feel angry at God for allowing the death to happen. This target for anger can be OK for God is big enough to take our wrath and deal with it. Anger at God can also be helpful in that it is an outward expression of rage, which can release the emotional force of our anger and dissipate it. Sometimes the deceased person can be in the firing line. This can arise when the mourner feels angry with the dead person because by dying in effect, they walked out on the mourner and left them high and dry. The mourner feels deserted and all alone with all life's problems to face without the help of the loved one, who now has none of these problems. It can arise especially if the loved one has left behind financial or other difficulties which have to be sorted out. There may be anger at the loved one, for example, for not taking advice and going to see the doctor sooner before it was too late. Anger at ourselves can be particularly intense should we have been in some way directly involved in the death. For example, we were driving the car involved in an accident resulting in the death of a loved one. In such cases, counselling should be sought immediately.

In other circumstances, we need to take a cold hard look to see if our anger is justified; usually, it is not. By talking over our feelings with others and hearing their point of view, we will come to a more balanced opinion. This gives us, for example, the opportunity to see that, in the circumstances, all that could have been done was done to treat our lost loved one. We need to think logically and openly and talk to friends and relatives about all the factors surrounding the death. Then we will come to realise that those caring for our loved one could have done no more than they did in the face of that fatal illness. In all of this, we must remember that our thoughts and feelings in the depths of grief are more often than not driven by emotion rather than logic.

Anger is a perfectly normal and natural emotion to be found being expressed when someone grieves the loss of a loved one. When it is turned outwards then typically there is no concern whatsoever. As the person journeys through grief, their anger will play itself out healthily and naturally. Should, however, that anger be turned inwards then this is when there is a real cause for concern. For anger, turned inwards can result in psychological damage. It arises from an irrational blaming of oneself as being in some way directly responsible for what has happened or for not being able to prevent the death.

Our feelings can lead to irrational outbursts of anger. Or it can leave anger bubbling under the surface of all we say or do. It can cause other people to give us a "wide berth" resulting in the loss of relationships with relatives and friends and other social contacts. It can also result in physical harm if the inward turning of our anger seeks an outlet through self-harm or in very extreme cases, even suicide.

This anger can be reasoned through, or it can find outward expression through being openly admitted to and talked through with friends or relatives. It will dissipate itself as we journey through grief. However, it may from time to time resurface later in our lives. These later re-occurrences need not cause concern so long as they too in a similar manner find outward expression. Thus they can be regarded as part of our natural progress through grief.

Anger becomes a cause for concern when it becomes turned inwards resulting in self-harm or attempted suicide. Or when it is expressed in destructive tendencies, such as smashing cups and throwing things about the house and elsewhere, in anger and possibly endangering other people. These damaging actions also include punching holes in doors or walls or windows, or lashing out verbally or physically in rage at members of our family or friends with little or no provocation or withdrawing into ourselves to fume alone with anger. These are all signs that our wrath is no longer natural and healthy. It is no longer naturally dissipating itself and help from appropriate professionals; for example, doctors or counsellors need to be sought.

People who are prone to outbursts of anger in their normal lives may also succumb much more readily to such outbursts of anger as they grieve. People who have a calm disposition may not so readily succumb as they can control such emotions in their normal lives.

Blame

Just as is the case with our anger, blame can be directed at many people and for many reasons. These include, for example, the surgeon because the operation failed, doctors or nurses whom you thought didn't do enough. Yourself, because for example, you didn't ensure that the deceased went to see a doctor immediately when they first complained of the initial signs of the fatal illness. The list of the blame game can go on and on. It will be directly linked to the particular circumstances leading up to the death. If it takes control of us, then it can have the same detrimental effects as anger. All of the advice given on seeking help in the case of anger is also applicable to blame. Usually talking over how you feel with a trusted friend followed by careful logical thinking will reveal that no one is to blame. You will come to see that everything was done that could reasonably have been done in the prevailing circumstances based on what was known at the time.

Rage

Rage occurs when anger and blame move up a gear and become a rage. In such cases then help must be sought from a doctor or counsellor. The advice given in the case of anger also applies to rage.

Resentment of other people.

This arises from the feeling that other people are getting on with their normal lives while you are plunged into grief. Resentment may be directed at particular individuals or people in general. This feeling may be enhanced as you compare your situation with, for example, notorious criminals who are not suffering as you, who are law-abiding and innocent. These emotions give rise to feelings of "I have done nothing wrong, so I don't deserve this." Talking your feelings through with a trusted friend will help you see things in their real perspective. It will enable you to understand that death calls on whoever it wishes irrespective of personal behaviour and circumstances. Should the intensity or persistence of the feeling of resentment cause you or your friends and relatives concern then help should be sought from a doctor or counsellor.

Hate

Resentment may, in exceptional circumstances turn into outright hatred of certain other people. It can arise out of jealousy because they are happily getting on with their lives unhindered. At the same time, you have to bear the significant burdens which grief can bring unfairly. In this case, help should immediately be sought from a doctor or counsellor.

Terror

The close contact with death which occurs on the death of a loved one can result in feelings of terror. In rare cases, this may stem from terror arising when you contemplate your death, which the death of a loved one has brought into sharp focus. Feelings of terror usually only arise where the death has occurred in exceptional circumstances. These include a terrorist attack or murder or a horrific car crash or accident. Terror can result from the thought that the same thing may happen to you or another loved one. Feelings of terror can come as you relive the circumstances of the death in the shoes of the deceased. Or your fear of death may turn into the more intense emotion of the terror of death. If these feelings arise, talking them through with a trusted friend is the best initial approach and visit a doctor or counsellor if this does not resolve your feelings or concerns.

Emotional Reflection giving rise to feelings of Guilt and Regret

Surprisingly when someone dies, we can feel guilt or regret on several counts. Should these feelings of guilt or regret cause you or your friends and relatives concern then help should be sought from a doctor or counsellor. Usually, this guilt or regret arises from the specific circumstances of the death and as such is not something which everyone who grieves experiences. Analysing your guilt or talking your feelings over with a trusted friend will enable you to see that your feelings of guilt are ill-founded. Additionally, we should be kind to ourselves, giving ourselves the benefit of the doubt. We should not be our own worst critics when feelings of guilt or regret surface in our grief.

If these feelings of guilt and regret persist, then help must be sort through a doctor or counsellor. Some of the forms of this guilt are as follows.

Guilt

Survival Guilt This can occur in anyone but is more usual, for example, where an accident involving several people results in 1 or 2 deaths. The survivors can feel guilty that they have survived when others have died. Logic tells us that this is irrational, but in grief, we tend to think with our emotions, not with logic. Such thoughts are irrational because who survives and who dies is out of the hands of the survivors. Survival depends on who was sitting where on the bus when the crash occurred. Survival Guilt can also arise in older people when a grandchild or someone young in the family dies. It gives rise to the feeling in the older person that it would have been better for them to die rather than one so young with all their life before them. Careful reflection reveals that such thoughts have no place in the real world for death calls on whom it will and when it will.

Enjoyment Guilt This is encountered when someone feels that by enjoying themselves, they are in some way letting down their loved one who has died. It is linked with the idea that as their loved one can no longer share in the joys of this life, then neither should they. Together with this idea comes the feeling that they should at all times, be feeling gloomy and depressed.

Careful thought should reveal to the mourner that as a result of their love for the survivor, the deceased would not wish this to be happening. The deceased loved one would not want to condemn the person who is grieving, whom they love, to a life of gloom and depression. Instead, they would wish them to enjoy themselves. It should also be remembered that enjoyment can also be a great antidote to grief.

Relief Guilt This is guilt resulting from a person feeling relief that someone, usually after a long and painful illness, has died. There are several possible sources for this feeling. It can stem from the fact that someone has wished for or maybe even prayed for the person who is terminally ill to be free from their suffering by dying. The death will, in turn, also release that person from the anguish of seeing the dying person suffer. The feeling of relief can stem from the fact that you no longer have to put yourself out in caring for the person now that they have died. This relief may also be felt because you no longer have to make a regular difficult journey to visit someone in a hospital. Or you no longer have to give up time and the things you enjoy doing to visit the terminally ill patient. Thus, when death occurs, there is a feeling of relief. As a result, the mourner feels guilty about the relief which they feel following the death. Such ways of thinking encourage the sense that the wish for or prayer for the deceased person to be free of their pain has, in some way, hastened and contributed to their death.

A moment's thought reveals that the relief felt is not something to feel guilty about but is, in fact, a demonstration of the love for the deceased. This love is revealed by the grieving person's feeling of relief for the person who has died for now their suffering is over. It shows that relief guilt is linked to the love felt for the deceased person.

Relief is a natural and healthy response in all aspects of life when we have felt under some kind of pressure which has then been removed. In the case of bereavement, it is the calm after the storm of seeing our loved one suffering as a result of their fatal illness. Feelings of relief are to be welcomed for they reveal the love for the deceased person as you identify with your loved one in gratitude that their suffering is over. It is the tranquillity and peace after the toil and heartbreak of caring for your loved one who was dying. That you undertook a burden for your loved one or friend during their terminal illness, for which you now feel relief at its release, reveals your love for your loved one. The feeling of relief is not an indication of your lack of love rather the opposite. The sense of relief does not mean that you would not give anything to have your loved one back restored to fullness of health. You now feel that a weight has been taken from your shoulders. Welcome this feeling for it will enable you to recharge your batteries and renew your inner strength. This, in turn, will help you on your journey through grief.

Regret When this feeling occurs in grief, it is usually linked to the particular circumstances of a death. The feeling of regret is represented in such statements as. "If only I had said he should take the bus instead of driving", following a death in a car crash. "If only I had rung for the ambulance sooner", following a death by a heart attack. Regret can also stem from not having said sorry for some passed hurt you had inflicted on the deceased. Or you may feel regret at not being able to say a proper "goodbye". Hindsight is a wonderful thing, but in life, we have to live without its benefits. So long as we tried our best in the circumstances and the knowledge we had at the time, then beating ourselves up with 'what if's' serves no useful purpose. If it persists, then regret can quickly turn to anger at oneself. Such anger, as we have already seen, can be one of the most damaging of emotions in these circumstances.

Should you have any of these emotions of regret. If you have any questions in your mind like "If only I had done such and such." Or you have things you would have liked to have said to your loved one, but could not pluck up the courage or did not have the opportunity, and now have feelings of regret or guilt. Then any or all of these regrets can be alleviated by writing a letter to the deceased expressing the issue you regret or the guilt. Then read it to yourself in private imagining that you are reading it to the deceased. Then still in private burn the letter and imagine that the heat and smoke rising is carrying the message upwards to the deceased person. They take with them all your feelings of regret. Or take these issues to God in prayer to ask for and receive his forgiveness for these and other "omissions" in your life. If you also wish, talk over these feelings of regret with someone you can trust, to see them into their right perspective. Do not allow yourself to become a martyr to these feelings. Or let the feeling of sadness become your link with your loved one. Should this happen then the help of a counsellor will be needed to help you to break this link.

First Aid in Bereavement

It must be emphasised that each person's grief is different. You may experience none or several of the emotions described above, which may suddenly burst on the scene or slowly build-up. All of these emotions which we have discussed here will be encountered on a person's journey through grief. They are a perfectly normal and natural reaction to the death of someone we love. They are the result of and a demonstration of that love. These emotions will naturally dissipate themselves overtime. This process can be aided by talking freely about these feelings to friends and relatives whom we trust. Listen to their views on our concerns and how we are feeling. This will help things to be seen in their real perspective. It helps us to appreciate better the reasonableness or unreasonableness of our feelings and outbursts. These conversations will be mutually beneficial should the other person be grieving also for the same or another loss. The dangers come when these feelings are bottled up and not naturally expressed by talking them over with someone you trust. Should these feelings persist for a longer time than is customary, or their intensity cause you or anyone else concern. Then help must be sought through a doctor or a counsellor.

Men and Women

Women are more outwardly emotional and therefore, more willing to talk about their emotions. This is facilitated by the fact that women have a circle of friends with whom they speak and share their feelings as a matter of course. Whereas men tend to have their mates with whom they don't share their emotions or concerns as a rule. They tend to talk about practical issues, for example, about sport or the relative merits of different cars.

Bereavement also reveals these emotional differences. Men and women grieve in different ways. In general, men often prefer not to show their emotions, and this applies to grief.

Men usually prefer to grieve alone and in silence, introspectively dealing with their feelings. This does not lend itself to expressing feelings and emotions; for example, men are reluctant to cry in public. It is a normal response for many men. Still, men need to be aware that what they are doing is not just refusing to acknowledge or hiding from their emotions by bottling up their feelings and emotions. Should this be the case, then they run the risk of building up a source of problems both now and in the future. Anyone who feels that they are running this risk needs to find someone with whom they feel confident to express their feelings and emotions. Perhaps join a bereavement group where they would be encouraged to do this.

Women are more at home with expressing their feelings and emotions in a variety of situations, which they do quite naturally amongst their friends in their everyday lives. They are, therefore, aware of the benefits of doing this. Thus, it comes intuitively for them to take this same approach when talking about their feelings and other issues connected with grief. It helps them to come to terms with their loss and eases their journey through grief. This is not to say that there will not be any overlap and some women will grieve in a similar way to men and vice versa.

These differences can be summed up in the word stoic. Men are stoic in the way they grieve preferring to simply take the impact of the death on the chin and then keep going. It is so because men prefer to deal with their emotions and thoughts inwardly and on their own. Then unwanted intrusions and enquiries into how they are feeling are likely to be repulsed, sometimes vigorously. This, for men, is normal behaviour but may mask the hiding away of grief. Should this be the case, then it can make it very hard to spot any problems or difficulties being experienced by such a man on their journey through grief. It arises because any such difficulties are being kept well out of sight.

# First Aid in Bereavement

An indicator that the grief is not being hidden away, and there are no problems or difficulties can be deduced from a person's behaviour. Should the man (or indeed woman) in question be sleeping and eating customarily. They are going out and socialising with friends as they usually would and are willing to speak about, and share memories of the lost loved one. Then this is a good sign that they are routinely coping with their grief. There are no problems brewing which will need to be addressed before they erupt at a later date (see Chapter on 'Normal Signs that a person is coping with their Grief'). If on the other hand if there is concern that these healthy behaviours are not happening. Then the grieving person, man or woman, should be firmly directed to seeking help from a doctor or counsellor if they are not prepared to take this step for themselves.

Men also prefer to dissipate their grief in practical activities such as making the funeral arrangements, acting as pallbearers, acting as executors of wills or arranging for the sale of the house or disposal of furniture, should the death result in need for a house clearance or house sale.

Men are also more likely to fall prey to anger in their everyday lives than women. Anger may become a means of expressing their grief, as discussed earlier in this chapter. This anger can also predispose men to more readily taking up complaints or even legal action. Should they feel that the care and treatment of their loved one were not as they should have been.

In the first instance grieving in the ways described above for men, (and for some women), is perfectly normal and natural and if it is not causing any other problems should be accepted as such. If of course, it is causing worries, difficulties or concerns for the bereaved person or their friends and relatives. Then help should be sort through a doctor or a counsellor.

# 6 NORMAL EVERY DAY EMOTIONS

**Help in the understanding of how to manage our emotions released in bereavement can be found through examining how we manage the same feelings, though less intense, which also occur in our everyday life.**

We have discussed the emotions associated with bereavement. It must be pointed out that these emotions are not exclusive to a period of mourning, for they also occur in our everyday life. However, when they do, they are far less intense, much easier to manage and affect us for a much shorter duration than is the case when they occur as a result of the death of a loved one. By reflecting on how we handle the effects of these similar but less intense emotions, we are better able to manage these emotions when they arise more intensely in bereavement.

The emotions associated with bereavement can arise when we hear of any bad news. When their doctor tells a person that they have a life-threatening illness, their reaction may well be one of denial and disbelief. On telling someone that you have just lost your wallet or purse. The response of the person being told may well be one of disbelief and denial as they respond with a statement such as, "You are joking, aren't you?" Or just the one word "No!" Or a response of disbelief may also be elicited on the announcement of good news. The student on hearing that they have got three 'A*'s in their 'A' level exams may genuinely declare "I don't believe it!" As is the case with grief, the initial non-acceptance of the news shields us for the time being from the immediate full impact of the associated emotions which we know will follow.

# First Aid in Bereavement

Any bad news can leave us feeling stunned with the consequential feelings of shock and numbness. It is the case on being told that we have just failed our exams or that we have been made redundant.

Disorientation can be felt not only on hearing bad news but also good news. On hearing that someone is going to be married, the response may often be "I am so excited I don't know whether I am coming or going." This means that the person is confused and disorganised by the news. Similarly, a person, on hearing the bad news that they have lost their job, will also be left feeling confused and disorganised.

Wanting to be back into a restored broken relationship can lead to similar emotions to the searching and yearning of bereavement. In this case, they are at a much less intense level, than that which we experience for a deceased loved one. A broken relationship can also leave us searching and yearning for what has gone. We look at old photographs and think of happy times which we once shared with the person from whom we are now separated and estranged. Such yearning and searching can arise having moved away from an old address, perhaps because of work requirements. We search and yearn to be back in those old familiar surroundings.

When things go against us, or strange things happen to us, then we can experience distress and feel panic, anxiety or even fear. Misplacing a wallet or handbag opens the door to feelings of panic and anxiety and fear of what the financial consequences might be. Awaiting an interview or an exam can also bring on feelings of panic, anxiety and fear.

Intense emotional feelings in our ordinary lives can also have a tangible effect on bringing about physical or bodily changes. Thus, when we are deeply in love, especially in our teenage years, we can suffer from a lack of appetite and intense mood changes. We have the phrase that someone is feeling "lovesick", which comes from the feeling of sickness as a reaction to the deep emotional feeling of being in love. When faced with a significant operation, we can claim to feel physically sick in the face of what lies ahead of us, because of our deep emotional feeling, a mixture of anxiety and fear.

Emotional outbursts involving anger, terror, resentment, blame, rage and hate are met in everyday life. We feel anger if we are passed over for a job and may feel; "What have I done to deserve this". We feel resentment as others get on with their lives, and we struggle with relationship problems with our partner or spouse. We blame others where their mistakes or perceived mistakes have adversely affected us. Our dislike for someone can soon turn irrationally into hatred. There are times in our life when we experience terror through being caught up in something, which we do not understand or control. It might be a riot or bank robbery or a severe car accident, and we are overwhelmed by feelings of fear and panic.

As we reflect on our lives and our previous actions, we may have feelings of guilt and regret at what we have done and said in past situations. There may be feeling guilt where we have let someone down or regret that we did not act in a different and better way. A careful review of the situation may reveal that in the circumstances and within the knowledge we had at the time, we acted as well as we could. We realise that and our feelings of guilt or regret have no real foundation.

We are all familiar with the lows in our life when we feel sadness, loss and emptiness. This may be a passing phase, for example when our favourite football team has lost yet again. They may be more profound and more devastating feelings, such as those caused by the breakup of a relationship or friendship.

The whole spectrum of emotions to which we are subject to in our journey through grief is not new to us for we meet every one of them, all be it less intensely, on our journey through life. How well we handle such emotions in our everyday life may be an indicator of how well we can manage those more intense emotions when experienced in bereavement. To seek help and guidance, during the times when we find ourselves struggling with these emotions on our journey through grief. We may wish to reflect on what we did to help us cope and manage these emotions at other times in our life.

# 7 THE FIRST YEAR AND BEYOND

**The pain of the first year of the journey through grief can be eased through an understanding and awareness of what people commonly experience in that first year and beyond. Other chapters explain how these experiences can be managed.**

Everyone's journey through grief will be different for everyone's circumstances are different. So do not worry if your feelings are different from the ones which are mentioned here. Do not be concerned if they occur in a different order or on a different timescale. Some feelings may last twice as long or even longer than is the case for a friend who has also experienced a similar bereavement. The following is a thumbnail sketch of a typical route map for the arduous journey through grief. The aim is to provide reassurance that what is happening in your life is normal. It is similar to what everyone experiences at such times. The pace of travel on your journey through grief may be quicker or slower than has been outlined here. Therefore, I have set this first year in the context of more long-term experiences of bereavement. The first year of mourning is significant for it is punctuated by the many occasions when you will be doing something for the first time without your loved one. The doing of things for the first time without your loved one can be as every day as; having breakfast; going out of the house; returning to an empty house; doing the gardening; driving the car, or going shopping. Everything we do will inevitably at some stage be done for the first time without our loved one. It will also include more significant 'firsts' without our loved one such as birthdays, Christmas, and going on holiday. Advice

# First Aid in Bereavement

on how to manage these 'firsts' can be found in the chapter on 'What to do about Anniversaries.'

Your friends and relatives are the best-placed people to help you during this time. To maintain contact with them, it is necessary to return your life to normal, doing the things you usually do, as soon as you are able. If at all possible, continue with your normal activities as soon as the funeral has taken place. This includes returning to work and maintaining your usual social activities and interests. No hasty or long-term decisions should be made until at least a year has elapsed from the death, unless these are unavoidable and driven by very urgent financial or other very pressing individual circumstances.

Immediately After the Death to Six Months

The initial worry, which might be conscious or subconscious is; "Can I live or even just exist without my loved one?" The initial days/weeks are taken up with discovering that you can, which in itself may be a shock and which you may also need time to come to terms with or as might be said: "get over." You may discover, sometimes to your surprise that you can live without your loved one simply because you do. Though immediately after their death, you may have felt that you would never be able to. This new life may well feel devoid of all the joy which enthused your life with your loved one, but none the less your life moves haltingly on. Relatives and friends rally round in support and give encouragement. There is much to do following a death both practically and administratively. You have to be involved in the organisation of the funeral, inform official bodies, pay the bills, and do the jobs your loved one usually did. These activities keep you gainfully occupied if not entirely focused in the first few days. You have mounted the tightrope of bereavement and begun, like the trapeze artist, to cross to the other side.

Though in reality, you will never reach that other side until your life ends and you reach that other side to which your loved one has so recently crossed. Looking to the future, your journey through grief will take you to the end of your life. The depth and length of your periods of sadness will decrease as the months and years pass. The periods for which your life seems customary will lengthen until, perhaps some two or more years later, life seems reasonable, apart from occasional bouts of sorrow. Though in the first six months of your grief, there may be little sign of the depth of your sorrow beginning to subside.

Recalling or being reminded of your memories of your loved one during the first six months will plunge you into deep sadness. As the months go by, perhaps after a year or two, these memories will come increasingly tinged with nostalgia and thankfulness as the treasured memories of your loved one. For the memories of your loved one will remain with you for the rest of your life. This is how it should be because your memories are the tangible continuation of that love which exists between you. Those memories which in the first six months of grief can be so painful and full of sadness will over the years become filled with gratitude and nostalgia and feelings of joy and fulfilment.

The initial steps along the tightrope of bereavement will be faltering and hesitant. You will learn how to keep your balance and what to do and say to maintain that balance as the weeks pass by. You will gain in confidence and reassurance in answering questions such as; "How do you feel?"; "How are things going?" There will be times when you are ambushed by grief and have a wobble or even fall off the tightrope. During the first six months, you also learn how to remount the tightrope and continue your journey.

Emotionally you have to deal with your feelings in your life without your loved one as well as the emotions of others who also feel the loss. You will wobble and be knocked off balance in the first days and weeks following your loss by those emotions associated with bereavement, which are described in the chapter 'Emotions and Bereavement.' This is natural and normal and only to be expected as these emotions become more familiar to you. You learn how to mitigate their impact upon you better. You will live through the first anniversaries such as birthdays. This can best be done by planning activities as advised in the chapter, 'What to do about Anniversaries.' You can build-up strategies to mitigate against being ambushed by grief, though such ambushes may happen at any time. As the months pass by, you will grow in inner confidence in how to manage your emotions. This, in turn, helps your confidence in managing and resuming your ordinary life.

As the first six months following the death come to a close, you may begin to feel more isolated and feel your loss more keenly for, amongst other reasons, the following:

1 You are no longer thrown into contact with people through doing the necessary jobs and tasks which have to be done in the immediate aftermath of the death. Tasks such as arranging the funeral and contacting banks and building societies which kept you occupied and in contact with people are by now long passed, and life has returned to regular routines.

2 The level of TLC from your friends and relatives will have declined. They will be feeling by now that you are "over the worst" and that you will benefit from "standing on your own two feet." Plus, the fact that, of necessity, they have to pick up the reins of their own customary lives with their own families to look after. For these reasons, their support will understandably have begun to wane.

It is helpful to be aware of these two factors and to counter them by being prepared to initiate activities yourself. Doing things which you are interested in and which will bring you into contact with other people.

3 After about six months, you may also become aware of changes in your friendship patterns. People who had previously been very close to you may now become more remote and detached. Other people whom before you would have classed as acquaintances have been drawn much closer to you. The reasons for this are examined elsewhere in the chapter 'Normal Changes to Expect.' You only need to observe at this point that this is normal. It is to be expected for the death will have deeply affected not only yourself but also your friends and acquaintances. It will have changed attitudes and social relationships. In much the same way, that an earthquake or landslide would change irrevocable a familiar landscape.

On your journey through grief, especially during the first six months, be prepared to put yourself first. This may not seem to be the ideal Christian approach to life, but things are different during bereavement. You are naturally feeling low, and as a result of lacking your usual energy, you are not very assertive. This leaves you vulnerable to being dominated or badgered into doing things you find unhelpful or even what you do not want to do. By consciously putting yourself first, you counter this understandable vulnerability. Always ask yourself is this best for me. If necessary, give yourself time to think by saying "I don't feel I can make a decision now. I will let you know later." Or just say "No."

Six Months to One Year After the Death

The journey through grief can be likened to a hike over gruelling terrain. Over the first days, weeks and months,

# First Aid in Bereavement

your journey through grief is characterised by cliffs and steep climbs and scrambles. These can stand like barriers to your progress and have to be ascended. This challenging terrain is caused by all the emotions which beset someone in mourning, which can appear out of nowhere, seemingly blocking our route to routine life. These are described in detail in the chapter on 'Emotions and Bereavement.' We have to climb over and plot our course through these emotions as we come to terms with them. As we come to terms with these emotions, we can begin to find our own feet for the climb. For now, we are alone and can no longer call on the strength and support of our loved one. The first six months of your journey is characterised by ascending cliffs and steep climbs. The next six months to a year and beyond maybe something akin to a hard-uphill slog as you adjust to your new life without your loved one.

It is now the time, if you have not already done so, to be thinking about the future as well as getting all the immediate things in your life sorted out. Once you have journeyed through the immediate shock of your loved one's death, now some six months later, you will be beginning to get a feel for what this journey through grief feels like and entails. You will be coming to terms with some of its ups and downs. You will be beginning to get a better feel for how to progress along and keep your balance on the tightrope of bereavement. You will now be more aware that you are in a new situation, without your loved one, and are beginning a new life without your loved one. You will have slipped back into your normal activities and interests at least those you wish to continue in your new life. You will also be beginning to look to new interests and activities which reflect your needs as you set out on your new life. To this end perhaps another useful image to describe what you should be doing over the next six months or so is to see yourself as a butterfly floating in the warm summer sunshine from one flower to another, from one activity/situation to another, with no intention of permanently settling but reviewing and exploring possibilities for the future.

What activities and situations are open to you will be dependent on your particular situation and interests. If you are still in fulltime employment, then that will occupy the bulk of your time and energies. It will keep your mind occupied, and so provide a bulwark against being ambushed by grief. You will also have limited time for other activities. Should you be retired or not seeking employment, then you have time, as much as 24/7, on your hands. Look for appropriate activities to do as advised elsewhere in this book. Also be prepared to sting like a bee, to get the more immediate things in your life sorted out to your satisfaction and advantage.

I have already mentioned that your journey through grief involves beginning a new life. In very simplistic terms, following the loss of your spouse or partner, you are 21 again starting your adult life all over again. But this time with the added advantage of having the experiences of life from which you have already learnt. You also have the bonus that you can take all the time which you need to, in making those decisions which will affect your long-term future. Unless that is you have very pressing financial decisions or other decisions which need immediate attention. In making decisions, which will bring significant changes to your future life, it is as well to delay such decisions until at least one year has elapsed since the death of your loved one. This, for many people, will be a sufficient length of time for them to be moving on from the initial shock of the death of their loved one. They will also be forming ideas of how their life might work out in the future without their loved one. Anyone who has not reached this stage should think again about making any significant decisions until they have reached this stage in their journey through grief.

First Aid in Bereavement

A stage characterised by having the ability to think positively about all the choices, implications and possibilities for this new life.

Beyond the First Year

For a few people, living through the first anniversary of the death of their loved one finally brings home to them the reality of the death of their loved one. Thus, for them the first few days and weeks following the anniversary of the death can be one of the lowermost points in their journey through grief, as the reality of the loss is fully and finally accepted.

As you move beyond the first year since the death of your loved one you should be beginning to think through where you might be, or what you would like to be doing in five or ten years, but delay making any decisions. Instead, mull over your ideas and give yourself time to thoroughly review all the pros and cons of those choices and opportunities. As time goes by, in most cases, it will be immaterial whether you decide in one month or the next month or even in one year or in the next year. The important thing is that it is the right decision for you in securing what you want for your future. You are on your own now making decisions to suit only you. Like it or not, you are now beginning a new life without your loved one. The choices and responsibilities are yours alone. So, continue those things from your old life which you wish to and add any new dimensions to your new life which you want to. You are in charge, so relax, review the choices and make any decisions in your own good time. Giving yourself the time and thought to ensure that they are the correct ones and are something you want. By all means, listen to everyone's and anyone's advice but don't let anyone badger you into anything. Only do what you are sure is best for you and fits in with your plans and don't be afraid to say things like "It sounds like a good idea but I am not yet ready to decide on that just yet. I will give it some thought and make a decision later." Or "I have several things to sort out before I can decide on that." Such responses will buy you time to think through all the pros and cons.

The first year of your journey through grief is the most difficult. You have now lived through all your "first times", birthdays, anniversaries, significant events, etc., without your loved one. Advice on what to do on these occasions is given in the chapter on 'What to do about Anniversaries.' You have discovered that you can live without your loved one. You have learned how to live with your grief. You are now one year into your new life and have had the opportunity to begin to look at the possibilities of where that new life may lead. You have now come sufficiently to terms with the shock of your loss to start to lay down firm plans for your future. In laying down these plans, do not hesitate to put yourself first. Yes, your old life has been shattered, but your new life has many years to run (probably until you are 80 years plus). You must ensure that it is fit for your purposes and that timespan. You must be prepared for being ambushed by grief along the way, but these occurrences will become fewer and further apart as the months and years pass.

You are also learning how to carry your memories of your loved one with you. They are the link to that love which you have for one another. As time goes by, you must seek to recall these memories with nostalgia, gratitude and happiness. It will enable you to remember them at will knowing that they will fill you with appreciation and well-being as you reflect on those happy past times. In much the same way as you would reflect on happy past times shared with present friends and relations. It may take several years for this state of affairs to come about. Then you will be able to recall the memories of your loved one at will without being immediately plunged into sadness and sorrow.

The first anniversary of the death marks the end of the 'firsts' which you have to experience and to live through. Irrespective of how well we manage these occasions as each "first" is approached there will have been the inevitable uncertainty. For some, there would have been the fear of the unknown and the worry of how you would cope or how it would affect you. Now with all these 'firsts' behind you, you have the knowledge and experience gained from your first encounter with a "first time", however well or otherwise each one worked out. In light of these experiences, you are better able to plan and manage future anniversaries. You will go into them with added confidence and reassurance gained from the fact that you have survived them once. Stressful though the occasion might have been if you were content with the way a particular anniversary passed. Then it would be good advice to plan the same or similar activities for the second and future occurrences of that anniversary. Should a first anniversary have been particularly distressing, then it would be advisable to plan something different for the second anniversary. It should be based on activities which proved successful at other anniversaries.

It may have begun to happen earlier, but certainly, by the end of the first year, you will find that you are being treated routinely by your friends and acquaintances. TLC may be noticeably absent except on significant anniversaries. Others will by now have got over the shock of the death of your loved one and will have returned their lives to normal. They will assume that you have done likewise. That this has happened is all to the good. The fact that you are being treated normally helps you to fit into that normality so that you too can once again live normally. Should you be ambushed by grief, some may say to you; "Surely you've got over it by now?" Just quietly ignore such statements or reply disarmingly; "Yes, I am well on the way to getting over it." Even, though you may not be, what these people are really saying is; "I have got over it so should you."

Some people describe the first year of grief as going through the activities of living without any real enthusiasm or real joy. The first six months can feel as if you are a punch-bag for your own emotions arising from your grief. No long-term decisions should be made in this first year. No decisions should be made which will affect you beyond planning your next annual summer holiday or next Christmas whichever comes last.

The Second Year

For many people, the second year provides a time to reorganise their life. They are now able to take stock of the things that are going on in their life. Now is the opportunity to begin to reposition yourself in your new life. The time has come to start thinking about long-term decisions and commitments. All the firsts are behind you.

The Third Year

Typically the third year is characterised by the realisation that you have come to terms with your grieving. Now, though you will still be subject to times of grief, you will no longer be overwhelmed by it. You are also noticeably repositioning yourself in your new life. You are actively progressing in the building of your new identity and a new life without the presence of the loved one who has died. You will carry with you your memories of your loved one and their influence on you for the rest of your life. Now is the time to firm up any long-term or life-changing decisions after careful thought and consultation with those who are closest to you!

It must be remembered that the process of grieving is necessary so that healing can take place. For the majority of people, the first year following the death of a loved one is the worst. During that year, you have lived through all the anniversaries for the first time. The succeeding years will become more comfortable for you to manage, and you will become less subject to being ambushed by grief. As the years pass by and grief subsides, there may be instances or even periods of intense grief of similar intensity to that experienced during the first year of grief. It can still occur 5 or 10 years or longer after the death of your loved one. As in many cases of being ambushed by grief, it may not be possible to isolate a particular reason why this has occurred. In some cases, there may be an obvious cause, such as an anniversary. If we know the reason, then we can make plans to avoid it happening again or mitigate its impact in the future.

Other causes may lie deeper within our mind. Nevertheless, being aware of them gives us the opportunity of controlling them and thus avoiding such intense grief. Such intense grief at a later time can be triggered as a result of still harbouring feelings of anger, blame, guilt or being hard done by. These have been discussed earlier but can linger in the mind to surface later. It maybe we see other couples talking over a meal out while we sit all alone. Perhaps we see other couples walking hand in hand, and we walk all alone. We are powerfully reminded of the loss of our partner. "I should be in that situation," we think. When we feel hard done by and are feeling low, we are easy prey to being overwhelmed by grief. If feelings of anger, blame or guilt persist, they can trigger intense grief if we allow them to dominate our thoughts.

Sometimes we sense our grief abating and with it feel we are losing our loved one all over again should we have allowed our grief to become one of or our sole link with our loved one. Thus, in an attempt not to lose that link, our grief may become more intense for a time. Being aware of these issues gives us the chance to assuage them as described elsewhere in this book.

Above all, it must be remembered that each person's journey through grief is unique. The above is only a sketch map to enable you to ascertain where you are on your journey through grief. If you are concerned that your journey is very much different from the one described, then seek help from your doctor or a counsellor.

# 8 MILESTONES ON THE JOURNEY THROUGH GRIEF

**Reassurance that your journey through grief is on the right track. It is achieved by noting the passage of the milestones which mark a typical journey through grief. It can help to bring calm.**

It is helpful to know the milestones which we shall pass on a typical journey through grief. Having such milestones in mind enables us to know that our passage is following its allotted course. They also reassure friends and family that our journey is on course. Some milestones will be passed simultaneously. The signs will be passed in roughly this order. However, there will be individual variations depending on the particular circumstances surrounding the death in question. For some these milestones may all be passed in 18 months to 2 years. For others, it may take 5 to 10 years. Each person's journey will be unique to them.

Significant Milestones

- Restore the stable eating and sleeping patterns that were there before the death of our loved one.
- To recognise and accept the fact of the finality of the death of the person who has died.
- To be able to continue relationships, and to establish new and good relationships with other people, to continue existing and make new friendships and acquaintances.
- Once more undertake and enjoy those experiences of life which we have always done, for example, holidays.

- To be able to talk about our departed loved one and to share memories about him/her with others.
- To appreciate that we are on a journey through grief.
- To be aware that grief is not something to recover from so that we can return to where we were before in our old life, as we would do in recovering from an illness. For as life returns to normality, we realise we are moving into a new life without our loved one.
- To be aware that we do not get over the grief and that grief will remain with us so long as we live and have memories.
- To be aware that as a result of journeying through grief, we are developing a new life and a new identity. There will be new meanings and new purposes for our life. While still retaining the influences of our loved one on our life and our memories of our loved one.
- To be able to live life without feelings of guilt and regret holding us back.
- To have control over the thoughts and memories of the person who has died, so that they do not preoccupy or dominate our thoughts.
- To be able to accept and welcome changes in our life.
- To be content with the way things are working out in our lives and not be attempting to make things stay as they were before the death of our loved one.
- To be aware of the new parts of ourselves, which we have discovered in our journey through grief.
- To be able to plan out our life for the future and look forward to that future life which we have planned. Ask ourselves what do I want to be doing or might I be doing in 5 or 10 years into the future and begin to make plans accordingly.

- To have adjusted to the new role we have in life as a result of the loss of the relationship we had with our loved one.
- To be fully aware, and understanding, of the fact that we have allowed ourselves to grieve and have journeyed through grief (some might say survived grief).
- To have become detached from our grief, so that we do not hang on to it as the last tie or link to our loved one and also possibly use it so that we can wallow in self-pity.
- To not panic or be anxious when we are surprised by grief, and a wave of intense grief once again passes over us. This grief may be triggered by memories, or at birthdays, or anniversaries or other occasions.
- To be able to deliberately reflect on our memories of our loved one, perhaps in some cases only after many years, looking on these memories with nostalgia, warmth, gratitude and happiness.
- To have come to realise that the pain of loss is an inevitable, healthy and natural part of living and results from our capacity to give and receive love.

Having passed these milestones, we come now to discuss our final destination. The journey through grief will last to the end of our life. Thus, our grief, though lessening in its impact, will always be with us. There will come a time, however, when our life feels normal again. This will, in a sense, be our final destination. This place in which we want to find ourselves should be characterised by memories of our loved one being recalled at will with nostalgia, gratitude and happiness. We should be aware that we have built a new life without the physical presence of our loved one, yet a new life deeply touched by their memory and influenced by their legacy. It may take two or three years or a decade, depending on the individual circumstances of our loss. The final ending of our earthly journey, the last days and hours of our own life's journey, dependent on our faith, may be characterised by looking forward to once again meeting with our loved one in God's nearer presence.

This list of milestones is not intended as a tick list to be visited daily to see if there is anything else to tick off. Nor is it to be used as a comparison chart to check if you are making better progress than is someone else. The milestones are listed to give a feel for how each person's journey through grief will progress. How quickly you reach each milestone and the precise order in which you do so will vary from individual to individual. After 18 months of the journey, many people will have passed most of these milestones or be aware that they are on their timetable to be passed shortly. For some of the later milestones, it may be five or more years before you are passed them.

This list should make you feel secure in the knowledge that passing these milestones is a normal and natural part of your journey through grief; however long this takes. As you pass them, you will know for yourself that your journey through grief is taking its usual course. You are on the right route. It should bring a measure of reassurance and support and give you self-confidence on your journey.

# 9 NORMAL CHANGES TO EXPECT

**We can be reassured through the realisation, that the changes which are taking place in our life, as a result of our loss, are healthy and to be expected.**

The loss of a loved one brings with it many changes to the lives of those who mourn that loss. The changes that occur are normal and to be expected. Many of these changes come about because the loss of a loved one brings about many other losses. The most noticeable and apparent changes come about as a result of the loss of the physical presence of our loved one and all that that means. There are however other losses, some of which may be unexpected until the changes which they bring are felt. The changes which these losses bring are routine changes and to be expected after the loss of a loved one, especially should this be a spouse or partner. Through the loss of your loved one, you will lose someone who has been a close confidante and friend. You may also lose some of your social life and some of your friends. You may lose work colleagues if you need to change jobs for financial or other reasons as a result of your loss. You may lose your self-reliance, your bubbly personality, or your sympathetic nature. You should be prepared to lose the old you which will, of course, be replaced by the new you.

The one loss and its accompanying changes which often goes unnoticed, at least in the first few months, is the loss of the old you. The loss of a loved one changes you in so many different ways. Primarily you lose your innocence. Before the death of a loved one, not only do you feel that this could not happen to me, but it never even crosses your mind that it could happen to you. Without warning after the death of a loved one, whether it is suddenly or after a long illness, you know full well that it can happen to you. Your innocence is swept away. Your innocence in the sense that life is good and will deal you no unexpected tragedies, especially if this is the first time you have lost someone close to you.

The old you also changes in that from now on you have to rely on yourself which will mean a new you. Your new you is a more self-reliant person. It is particularly so in the case where the deceased is a spouse or partner. No longer do you have someone to bounce ideas off before making a decision. No longer do you have someone trusted, close to, and confidential. They give you the benefit of their experience and advice and with whom you can share your deepest concerns and thoughts. No longer do you have someone who will support and encourage you come what may. Now, because of this loss, you have to be a new you. In this, you experience the loss of the old you. To a lesser extent, this is also the case with the loss of a parent. In the case of the loss of a parent, you may immediately begin to fear that you may lose your remaining parent. Even though before the death, the thought of even losing one of your parents might never have entered your head. You have been irreversibly changed. You are now fully aware of your mortality and the mortality of those nearest and dearest to you.

The effect of the loss and the changes it brings will vary depending on individual circumstances. In the case of the death of a parent, these changes will be most noticeable, the closer the relationship with the deceased parent. Should this parent have been the one whom you most readily gravitated towards. For they provided you with the most advice and were your touchstone for your on-going life. Then the change from the old you will be the most drastic. For now, you have to be more self-reliant and make decisions without the help and advice of that parent. It will take time to establish the same sort of relationship for your remaining parent will be caught up in their grief. It will make this process more difficult. You will have lost the one person who gives you the most support and encouragement in your life. This loss of support and encouragement can undermine your confidence and be debilitating for you in your everyday life. You need to become a new you either finding someone else to replace the deceased person or coping on your own or a combination of both. There will be changes in your confidence levels. There will be changes in the roles required of you.

It may come as a surprise to discover that your relationships with your friends are also changed as a result of the death of a loved one. Should that loved one be your spouse or partner, then the death will plunge you back into the life of a single unattached person. You no longer have the security of marriage or a fixed partner to identify you as someone having a secure and stable relationship. Safe in this relationship, you are protected from the uncertainty and insecurity of the attentions of the opposite sex, particularly those who are single and unattached. Friendships with the opposite sex were managed and controlled by your marriage status, or your being in a relationship. These are now changed into a more fluid less predictable and a less regulated and directed relationship. What had been a stable and fruitful friendship with a single person of the opposite sex may disintegrate in the face of these new pressures and demands. These new pressures may come directly from the person involved who now wishes to deepen this erstwhile friendly relationship when you do not want to. Tensions may arise through others who perceive a need for you to form a new relationship. They arrange, with other eligible single people, meetings and situations to promote this perhaps against your better judgement. This loss of old relationships could result in the loss of old and valued friends.

Relationships with married couples and those with a stable partner are also affected. When going out as a couple, with another couple, no longer is it a stable foursome of two married couples or partnerships, with inter-relationships clearly defined. Such a friendship/relationship has now become a relationship involving three people in which you are the other woman or man. You may become a possible cause for unbalancing the stable relationship which the other couple has. You may be perceived correctly or incorrectly as a rival in the camp. How this plays out will determine your long-term closeness in this new situation and whether such a friendship will be maintained over the coming years or not as the case may be. Should the new dynamics of the relationship become sufficiently changed and soured. It could gradually diminish or rapidly terminate friendship with another couple which had previously gone on for many years.

In the case of the death of a parent, the most significant impact on their friendships will be felt by children and teenagers rather than adults who lose their parent. For many children or teenagers, sympathetic friends will ensure that life with them goes on as usual. There are, however, many pitfalls to this smooth transition. A child who has had the particular support and encouragement, and been actively aware of this, of the deceased parent, may with their loss, become less confident and more withdrawn. It may consciously or subconsciously be picked up by their friends and result in changing relationships which may lead to the grieving child becoming detached from their friends. Should this effect be very severe, the grieving child may choose to withdraw from these friendships altogether. It could lead to time spent time alone in their room rather than playing with their friends. Thus, in addition to the loss of a parent comes the loss of friends and companionship.

It may also arise from changes in the disposition of the person who has lost a loved one. Thus, a child/teenager who was bubbly and outgoing may now become quiet and tentative or withdrawn—friends who were drawn to that person because of their bubbly and outgoing nature. May, with no malice, be drawn to other bubbly and outgoing people leaving behind their old friend. Alternatively, a friendship based on the fact that the person who has lost their loved one, was a steady-going type may fade away. It can happen should the loss of their parent turn the steady-going type into a risk-taker. Who now starts to associate with other risk-takers and frequents risky places, or takes to fast motorbikes or cars. These changing friendship patterns may be of concern to the surviving parent, for the new friends are unknown. They have not had their dependability and reliability tested over time as have old friends.

Also, it must not be overlooked that some children, who have lost a parent, maybe bullied. Their loss has resulted in the loss of libido. They are generally feeling low. This can make them a natural target for bullies, for they now have no energy with which to fight back. Such children are just what bullies are on the lookout for. Some children simply being reminded of the death of their parent will immediately plunge them into tears and sadness, the result for which the bully is looking. This might be done simply by the bully mentioning, seemingly in all innocence, that they thought that they had just seen the dead parent walking down the street. The bereaved targeted child may also have lost their friends for reasons outlined above. They now have no close support and are on their own and isolated and an ideal target for bullies. Those caring for children in this situation need to be fully aware of this vulnerability to being bullied.

Acquaintances and friends will have been made. As a result of the type of work in which your deceased partner was involved. There would have been the work's social gatherings and other links to the work of the deceased. These will now stop or at least change in frequency, and it is inevitable that these friendships, or at least some of them, will be lost. What will also be missed is the experience of attending such gatherings which may have constituted a large part of your social life with your spouse or partner. You may also lose the status of being the partner of the person holding a distinguished position at work. Thus, diminishing and changing your social standing. How this will affect, you will vary from person to person.

Attendant on the physical loss of a partner is a whole host of emotional losses. Suddenly you are without a confidant, a shoulder to cry on, a helper with the children, a supporter and encourager, someone who picks you up when you are down. You lose the entertainment and fulfilment you received in doing things with your partner. It might have been supporting and going to the matches of your local football team or attending the theatre or concerts or playing bowls together. There would also be more personal activities like holidays and celebrations, such as Christmas, done together. Now you must do and face these situations alone. It will inevitably lead to more stress in your life.

There may also be material changes if the deceased was the primary or only breadwinner. Now, less money will be coming in, and this may need more careful budgeting. It will result in a variety of material losses together with a loss of the certainty of financial security which may have pertained before the death. These financial worries will take time and effort to plan around as well as the extra emotional stress of dealing with them.

Should the surviving partner have to return to work. This will result in the loss of freedom resulting from not having to work. There will also be the loss of friendships, companionship and activities as a result of having to return to work. Nevertheless, on the positive side, there will be introductions to new working colleagues which will enhance the social scene.

The death of a parent who is the only, or one of the breadwinners will inevitably lead to changes as a result of less money being available to the family. This could lead to a downsizing of the home where a mortgage has to be financed or to less material goods and pleasures in life, which will also affect children. It will include fewer toys, less technological and electronic gadgets and machines, as well as fewer clothes and changed holiday arrangements to fit in with the reduced budget. The extent of the losses and how they are received by the child(ren) will depend on individual circumstances.

The death of one partner can lead to the loss of relationships with the family of that partner. It can lead to less emotional and financial support and in the case of children a changing of their relationship with their grandparents and uncles and aunties. They may now see these people less frequently or perhaps not at all. This effect may be most significant should the surviving parent remarry or form another relationship, for then another new family may take their place. Thus, following on from the death of a loved one, there is not only the changing emotional landscape to be negotiated but also changes socially in the relationships with friends and relations.

There will be changes in the personality and behaviour of a person who has lost their loved one. These changes in behaviour will vary from person to person. The following questions will help you to assess how such changes are affecting you.

To assess the effects of your loss, you may wish to reflect on the following behaviours, which can be influenced by your loss. This assessment can be done by asking oneself these questions. In each case, compare the situation before your loss to how it is now, for example, one year, after your loss. Ask yourself these questions:

Has my loss:
Made me more confident or less confident?
Do I now feel more or less lonely?
Am I now a stronger or weaker person?
Do I now have more or fewer responsibilities?
Am I now more content or less content with my life?
Do I now enjoy my leisure time activities more or less?
Am I now more independent or less independent?
Do I now attend more or fewer leisure time activities?
Am I now a more caring or a less caring person?
Do I now get irritable more or less easily?
Am I now more impulsive or less impulsive, for example, in what I buy?
If you are a religious person:
Is my faith now weaker or stronger?

There may be other changes in your behaviour which you may notice have come about since your loss. In this case, a similar questioning of the situation before and after your loss will help you to assess the impact of your loss. Of course, some of your answers may be that no noticeable change has come about. There are no right or wrong answers. This process will also allow you to assess your progress if you compare your feelings say two and three years after the loss with one year after the loss.

Should you be concerned about a friend or relative who has lost a loved one. Then by asking yourself such questions of others, you can also assess the impact of their grief on their behaviour

It can be particularly helpful in the case of evaluating the effects of grief on young children/teenagers following the death of a parent or close relative. If appropriate and useful, you can ask the questions directly of your friend or relative if they agree. Then if helpful, discuss their answers. You will then have to decide how to proceed should any concerns be revealed.

The usefulness of this process is to be found in indicating to you any changes or aspects of your new life, which may be of concern to you. Should any concerns be uncovered then, the next step is to ask yourself how you need to adjust your lifestyle, to seek to alleviate them. Should the answers reveal any significant concerns or worries about your changed behaviour, or that of someone else, seek the help of a doctor or counsellor.

# 10 NORMAL SIGNS THAT A PERSON IS COPING WITH THEIR GRIEF

**It is reassuring to know that our journey through grief is taking a typical course.**

Difficult though the journey through grief is, some 80% to 90% of people successfully make this journey with the help of their friends and relatives. 10% - 20% of people may need the help of a counsellor who may be sought through a doctor or organisation such as Cruse Bereavement Counselling. However, there are no accurate statistics kept on this matter.

Confirmation that a person is coping well with their grief can be found in the fact that they are eating and sleeping as they did before the death. They are maintaining their standards of appearance, tidiness and presentation as they would have done in the months before their loss. Further, the bereaved person can talk about and is willing to talk about their loved one and their memories of them as and when the subject crops up in normal conversation.

The journey through grief will inevitably contain times of tearfulness and deep sadness. These are the natural human responses to the death of someone we love. They should be recognised as healthy and natural and to be expected. These times will come and go throughout mourning being more frequent and more intense at the beginning and gradually becoming less frequent and less severe as the months and years pass. They may well re-emerge from time to time, even many years into the future, perhaps triggered by a memory or a photograph, a sound or even a smell. It is the way of grieving. This deep sadness will vary from person to person. Its form will be dependant on the personality of the mourner, the closeness of their relationship to the deceased and the factors surrounding the death.

A person is coping with their grief if the answer yes is given to the following questions. That the answer is yes, indicates that the person is managing well and should continue to do so with the continuing support and help of friends and relatives around them.

You can, of course, ask the same questions of yourself if you have suffered the loss. In the immediate aftermath of your loss, you may well be too occupied just coping with your grief to have the time or energy to answer such questions. You will feel better able to do this for yourself as time passes.

- Is the person eating and sleeping as they usually do?
- Is the person looking after themselves in the sense that they present themselves to the world thoughtfully dressed and clean and tidy? As they would have done before their loss.
- Is the person keeping their house/room as clean and tidy as they would typically do?
- Is the person still socialising, going out and meeting the people as they usually did and going to the places they customarily visited?
- Is the person open to and meeting new friends to establish new friendships?
- Does the person talk about their lost loved one and share memories with others about him/her?

If the answer to any of these questions is no then gentle help and encouragement should be applied to enable a change in behaviour so that the answer changes to a yes. If there is no response to this encouragement, then professional help needs to be sort from a doctor or counsellor.

Is there a lessening in the intensity of the grieving and a decrease in the number of occasions when deep sadness is felt? It also indicates that someone is coping with their loss.

As your journey through grief progresses beyond a year, there are two questions which can be asked, which will help measure the progress a person is making. These questions are:

1. Is the mourner now being ambushed by grief more or less frequently than was the case 6 months and a year ago?
2. Is the mourner now crying more or less often than was the case 6 months and a year ago?

The answers here should indicate a decreasing frequency though there will be ups and downs along the way.

It must be emphasised that every individual case of bereavement will work out in its particular way. It must also be remembered that there may be a "one-off" time or times of intense grief at any time during the journey through grief.

# 11 SIGNS THAT A PERSON IS STRUGGLING TO COPE WITH THEIR GRIEF

There are signs to look out for, which indicate that a person is not coping well with their grief. This suggests that the help and support of friends and relatives are not enough and that it is imperative to call in professional advice from a doctor or counsellor.

These signs are not an exhaustive list. Professional help needs to be sought if you have any concerns whatsoever that your friend or relative is not coping with their grief. Or that you are not dealing with your grief. If you are the one who has suffered the loss, these signs will also apply to you. It may well be that you are so caught up in your grief that you are unable to acknowledge and respond appropriately to these signs. In which case cooperate with friends or relatives who are trying to help you.

A person, who is not coping, for whatever reason with their grief, may well display the following behaviours. Should the answer to any of these first four questions be yes, then professional help needs to be sought immediately. It can be done by contacting a GP, other health professionals, Cruse Bereavement Counselling, or Samaritans. Advice needs to be found quickly for the grieving person, with or without their consent. You may need to accompany the bereaved person to the first meeting. There you can inform the professional helper of the full situation and circumstances. Taking their advice as to what you might be able to do to help. If you are the bereaved person, then you can ask yourself these questions. You may also likewise wish to take a friend or relative with you to your first meeting with a professional. If the answer is yes to any of these questions, then help must be sought immediately as is indicated above.

As a direct result of the death, does the person who has suffered the loss:

- Self- harm?
- Threaten suicide?
- Undertake excessive drinking of alcohol or taking drugs (illegal drugs and/or medical drugs to promote calm or aid sleeping)?
- Suffer from deep depression and ceases to interact with others and withdraws from old activities and friends?

That a person is struggling to cope with their journey through grief is revealed by the answer yes to any of the following questions. Professional help must again be sort as outlined above if the behaviour is causing distress or concern to the mourner or friends and relatives. It is particularly so if the bereaved person is showing no definite signs of improvement as time passes by and especially so if any of these conditions continue beyond six months from the loss. These issues will also apply to yourself if you are the person who has suffered the loss.

Does the person:-

- Exhibit excessive moodiness, anger, guilt or anti-social behaviour?
- Suffer from illnesses which could be labelled as psychosomatic?
- Display severe and intense sadness at the very mention of the dead person?

- Refuse to talk about the dead person and share collective memories of them?
- Keep the dead person's belongings and/or leave their room unchanged?
- Keep up the appearance of being unaffected by the loss (this may indicate a denial of the death or unnaturally postponing grieving)?
- Become very active in doing a variety of things almost to the point of exhaustion? It may indicate being proactive to postpone the sadness associated with, and the ensuing journey through, grief. They thus deny themselves of the benefits of the healing which grieving brings.
- Launch into a new and very different pleasure-seeking lifestyle, possibly taking a new partner or multiple partners immediately or shortly after the death of a spouse or partner? It may indicate the taking on of distraction(s) to avoid having to grieve or there may be some other causes for this behaviour.
- Reject outright any suggestions of seeking counselling or help?

There may be other incidents which take place or patterns of behaviour which develop giving cause for concern precipitating the need to seek professional help and counselling.

Making judgements on these issues without knowing the full individual circumstances and without meeting the mourner is a problematic matter. Some of these behaviours may occur for a short time immediately following the death, or suddenly appear in isolation, and then subside. The real concern comes if one or more of them persist and show no signs of abating or changing.

If in doubt err on the side of caution and point the bereaved person in the direction of help, bearing in mind that the bereaved person may not welcome this. Go with your relative or friend on the first visit. It will ensure that the full circumstances of the bereavement and your concerns are revealed to the professionals concerned. It may be that in the case of self- harm or excessive drinking or drug-taking. The resulting contact with the emergency services will trigger the professional help and the opportunity for professionals to examine how you, or your friend or relative is coping with their grief. Help must be found to avoid this coming about.

# PART 2 WHAT TO DO

# 12 WHAT TO DO ABOUT GRIEF

**Support through useful first aid strategies to manage the effects of grief and its emotional impact on a person's life.**

To experience grief is a normal event in a routine life. We experience grief as a direct consequence of the love which we have for the person who has died. Unfortunately, there is no ready-made antidote to grief. There is no medication which can cure sorrow as a headache or toothache can be cured with the taking of medication or appropriate treatment. There are no ready-made phrases or sayings or activities which will automatically assuage our grief. The best way in which we can help ourselves is to resume our routine life as quickly as possible. This would include returning to work and undertaking our usual social and leisure meetings and activities with friends and relatives. It will ensure that we maintain contact with our friends and relatives who are the best people to provide help and support during this difficult time. In more detail, the following suggestions will help to mitigate grief's worst excesses.

1. Keep your life as habitual as possible. In doing this, you will provide yourself with the reassurance which comes from the security of knowing that things are going on as they always have. Keeping your mind and your life occupied ensures that you are less open to the possibility of being plunged into grief. Most importantly maintaining life's old routines will keep you in contact with your friends and family and work colleagues. They are the best-placed people to support and help you at this time. Do the everyday things as you have always done and make your usual plans for the future like planning holidays. If at all possible,

# First Aid in Bereavement

continue to fulfil any plans you had already prepared for the future before your loss, provided they are not life-changing.

2. Seek out a friend, or relative, or counsellor if you feel it necessary to whom you can openly talk about your grief and share your worries or concerns.

3. Take one step at a time. Take one hour at a time. Take one day at a time. You will be too emotionally exhausted to do anything other than this in the initial stages of your journey through grief. Also be prepared to fall back on this strategy later on in your journey through grief, if you begin to feel emotionally exhausted.

4. Accept that you are going to be ambushed by grief, but be prepared to limit its effects. Through experience, you will learn how to handle and control these overwhelming feelings of sadness. It gives rise to the notion that time heals grief, but in reality, it is, that over time, our minds learn how to manage these emotions. Avoid circumstances which are an open invitation for grief to ambush you. These circumstances will vary from person to person and will become apparent if you are not already aware of them. They include attending a funeral too soon after your loss. In such circumstances, feel free to explain that this is the reason why you could not participate in the funeral. If you are ambushed by grief, be prepared to withdraw from the situation, (go to the toilet or similar quiet place) to regain your composure. Or make an excuse that you need to return home. It will allow you to gain your composure in the car, before going home. Do not drive while crying or overcome by grief.

5. When you feel strong enough, face your grief possibly through a quiet time on your own, in your room, in your garden or elsewhere where you feel safe and secure. Then

reflect on the good times you spent with your loved one. Set yourself a time limit maybe 10 minutes, half an hour at the most. This avoids triggering a whole afternoon of grief. Have something to do at the end of 10 minutes or whatever time you set. It can be to watch a TV programme or DVD or to go out shopping. This helps to ensure you keep to your time limit. As you think of the past times with your loved one, aim to look on them with gratitude, not sadness. If you are strong enough, use photographs to remind you of these good times.

If you wish to visit the places you once enjoyed visiting with your loved one to help recall memories. Or visit places which help you to reflect such as beaches or moorland. Again, set yourself a time limit for how long you wish to be there. Be aware that lonely, isolated places can leave you vulnerable to attack. Go to these places (moors, beaches, etc.) to grieve with someone else, walk with them or leave them in the car if you wish to be alone, but stay in visual contact.

6. Develop havens where you can go, knowing you are unlikely to be surprised by grief. You may already have some in mind. These will normally take the form of new people to be with, new interests and new places to visit which have no associations with the person who has died. To enable this to happen, for example, you may wish to join the local poetry group or quilting group or tennis club or visit National Trust properties or RSPB sanctuaries or take up other new interests or hobbies in your life.

7. Do not be afraid to cry. Crying is one of our natural healing processes. If you feel a 15 minutes cry coming on, don't stop after 10 minutes because you feel you ought to. It's impossible to cry forever, though you might feel that that is what you want to do. On each occasion that you cry,

you will cry your last tear, and that will leave you with a calmness which is beyond understanding.

8. Everyone's grieving is different. You are the only expert on your grief for only you know its full extent and those things which ease your pain. Nobody else can be an expert on your grief or advise you against your better judgement. Be quietly and inwardly proud to be grieving. It is a natural and normal response to the loss of a loved one and shows your love. Grief is one of the links to the love which you shared with your loved one. But do not allow your grief to be or become your only link. For then, your grief can come to dominate your life, and you fail to move onwards in your life. The situation can arise that it is only in grieving and when you are sad that you come to feel close to your lost loved one. This relationship of sadness is not what your loved one would want, nor is it in your best interests. Far better links are memories, which bring you feelings of gratitude, contentment and happiness. Initially, your memories of your lost loved one may well be/will be tinged, to a greater or lesser extent, with sadness. But over the coming months and years, your memories will change and mellow to bring you feelings of gratitude, contentment and happiness.

9. Always be prepared to put yourself first to counter your vulnerability to being dominated or bullied because you may be naturally feeling low. Often in grief, you are without your normal levels of energy and assertiveness and so vulnerable to being persuaded to do something, not in your best interests. Ask yourself before doing anything "Is this the best for me?" In answering this ask and reflect on what those closest to you might say or think and what your departed loved one would think.

10. Be prepared to delay decision-making. Give yourself time. In the case of any big decisions to make you need to

give yourself time to think. These big decisions include moving house, especially if it is away from friends and neighbourhood; career or job change; new partner or close relationship. Unless pressing urgent financial or other need. You need time to think and time to plan. It might need to be a year or two following the death if it will affect your future and be in any way life-changing. Certainly, as a general rule, there should be no big decisions taken in the first year. No hasty decisions at any time, especially those which might affect the next few years or the rest of your life which with increasing longevity may well be to beyond 80 years.

11. Be prepared for anniversaries (see the chapter on 'What to do about Anniversaries').

12. Accept that the death of a loved one inevitably means that you now have to build a new life without them. The death of a spouse or partner leaves you single once more with all that that means. You will still carry your loved one into your new life through your memories and the influence they have had on you. You are 21 again but without the energy and expectations of a 21-year-old. However, you do have a lifetime of experience to draw on.

13. Let your mind and body lead you. The impact of grief on someone's life can be compared with the impact of a severe operation after which we can be left physically exhausted and mentally and emotionally all at sea. After a major operation, we need to listen to our minds and bodies and what they are telling us. Our bodies will tell us when we must rest. Our minds will tell us when we need rest and recuperation for our thoughts and emotions. We would treat this as normal after a major operation. Do likewise with grief. In just the same way let your mind and body lead you. Take the time you need to recuperate. Don't be afraid to wrap yourself in cotton wool, if need be, as you

would after a major operation. As with a major operation, there is the need, as soon as possible, to be out and about exercising and socialising as you normally would.

14. Be prepared for men and women to grieve differently (see the chapter on 'Emotions and Bereavement'). Women tend to be more open with their grief and, so grief is dissipated in a normal and natural manner. Men, who tend to be not so open, need to be aware that they are not bottling up their feelings and emotions. Such action may lead to becoming the source of problems either now or in the future. If this is the case, then men need to find someone to whom they can express their feelings and emotions, perhaps joining a bereavement group where they would be encouraged to do this. Failing this, they may be in more need than women are to seek the professional help of a doctor or counsellor.

We cannot just switch off grief when it sweeps over us. Taking the above steps are the best way to exercise some control over it and reduce its opportunities to ambush us.

# 13 WHAT TO DO ABOUT ANNIVERSARIES

**Some first aid suggestions of activities to do on anniversaries which will help to ensure they do not become grief-ridden days.**

Bereavement changes some anniversaries from dates to be looked forward to, to dates to be dreaded. If we are not careful, then anniversaries can leave us wallowing in grief. To ensure that anniversaries do not become grief-ridden days, the first step a mourner should take is to put themselves first. Be good to themselves, for this is what your loved one would want for you. It is best achieved by doing those things which will best enable you to manage your grief on these dates. With this in mind, it is advisable to ensure that activities are planned on these dates. It will keep the mind occupied and so guard against being grief-stricken or ambushed by grief. These activities should be different from the ones which have been done in the past with your loved one and are traditionally associated with that anniversary. The same or similar activities run the risk of continually reminding oneself of the loved one and being plunged into grief as a result. If you feel strong enough, time can be set aside, perhaps 10 minutes or half an hour at the most, to reflect on your loved one in the light of that special anniversary and what it meant to both of you.

It has been mentioned elsewhere that our journey through grief can be likened to recovering from a major operation. In the case of recovering from major surgery, we would take great care in planning what we were to do each day. We will be especially careful not to overtax ourselves or undertake anything which might cause us undue stress. This is also the case on our journey through grief. It is essential to plan. We must ensure that we are not going to do anything which will increase our stress or overtax us emotionally or plunge us into grief.

In life, it is always a good idea to prepare for future events. As an example, consider the situation surrounding a coming exam. You can try to forget about it and pretend it won't happen or you can prepare for it. A moment's thought reveals that preparing for it is the best course of action. Preparing for it gives you the best chance of getting the best outcome for yourself. If you don't prepare for it, then the day of the exam will inevitably come, and you will be in for a shock. Revise and prepare for the exam, and you will avoid that shock. You will also give yourself the best chance of getting a good result which will influence your future for the better. Similarly, it is a good idea to prepare for those days on which an anniversary falls in your journey through grief. You will, as is the case with an exam, increase your chances of getting a good result which will influence your future for the better.

The journey through grief is signposted by anniversaries. These anniversaries include those linked to the fatal illness for example; the anniversary of the death of your loved one, the anniversary of the funeral, the anniversary of first going into hospital and first being made aware of the seriousness of the illness. The traditional anniversaries celebrated throughout your life with your loved one. There may be individual ones and private and personal ones, places visited, and notable holidays shared. There will also be universal ones such as birthdays and wedding anniversaries. It is much better to prepare for these dates rather than to try to ignore them or just drift into them. It is especially so for first anniversaries.

As with anything taking place for the first time in our lives, there is the uncertainty, even fear, of the unknown. Think back to your first day at a new school, first day at work, first exam or first driving lesson. Before each one, we ask ourselves; "How will I cope?" "What will it be like?" In the case of anniversaries connected with the loss of a loved one, we will inevitably ask ourselves beforehand; "How will I cope?" "How bad, how sad, how hard, will this first time without my loved one hit me?" Once we have lived through, some might say survived, that first anniversary then, we approach that anniversary for a second time with the confidence that we have lived through it once. On the second occasion, we know what to expect. We now have the added experience of living through it once and recognise the emotions which the occasion releases. We also know what activities best helped us to ensure that those emotions did not overwhelm us. At the second anniversary, we are better prepared to avoid or manage those emotions. That is not to say there may be times when something unexpected happens, and we are caught off guard and ambushed by grief. In much later years, you will find it easier and come to look at anniversaries with nostalgia and gratitude. You will come to see that those anniversaries encapsulate all that your loved one meant for you.

If you do not prepare for these anniversaries, then you will leave yourself open to a day of grief. The following are some ideas which will help to prepare for and manage these anniversaries which will fall year on year. Most importantly, it is a good idea to have the whole day planned out with activities, akin to a school timetable. But this is a timetable which you can adapt and change at will. It is helpful to write down a strict schedule, with specific times, stating what you plan to do for that period on that day. Set out the time table to cover from getting up to going to bed. Put on the timetable everyday activities which you might be doing anyway. As the day unfolds, you do not need to stick to this timetable unless you wish to. You can, of course, retime your time table or fit in other different activities in the light of how the day is progressing.

If the date falls on a working day, then go to work as usual. The normality of work will be an excellent antidote to grief. You will be constructively occupied for most of the day. The regularity of the day will automatically reassure you that everything is as it should be. Even though a moment's reflection tells you it most certainly is not. This sameness of the day with all the other working days will also help to disguise its uniqueness from you. In effect, you get lost in what you are doing and in the normality of the day. Try to plan activities for the rest of the day or the whole day should it not be a day at work. In making your plans, it is OK to seek to explain to people close to you, that you are planning these activities as it will help you through the day, which is the anniversary of……. It will help them to understand what is happening. It will avoid any questioning, such as "why are you doing so and so?". Or "you don't usually do that," which might lead to your being ambushed by grief, should the question catch you off guard. People will understand what you are doing and why. It will help others also in coming to terms with their grief which they maybe also feeling, which stems from the same or a different loss. It will also guide them as to what to do should they find themselves in similar circumstances on a journey through grief. It may be that you feel that it will not be so easy to explain to someone why you are doing this, as you may naturally hesitate to draw them into your grief. In this case, it is as well just to get on and plan and do the things as a matter of course without saying why you are doing it, and let things take their course. Should the occasion arise and someone asks you why you are laying these plans then explain why you are doing what you are doing.

Be open about the situation, and it will help you in coming to terms with your grief. Despite this planning, as the day progresses, you may feel overcome with grief. Should this happen, then withdraw to the ladies or gents (or similar). It will give you time to gather your thoughts once again and on returning explain that it is the anniversary of ............... and you were ambushed by grief. That you grieve and may want to cry on these occasions is all perfectly normal and natural. On the inside be quietly proud of your grief. It is, in one sense, the concrete evidence of the continuation of your love for the person who was died.

You have complete freedom in planning these activities, and they can include anything you wish. In the main, they will be everyday activities which you might be doing in any case. You also need to arrange to spend time with other people talking to them and doing things with them. This will include others who may also be feeling the same loss, and it will help them on their journey through grief. Ensure that the whole day is planned out. This limits the opportunities of being ambushed by grief. You should also plan in a coffee break or any other kind of break. Physical activities such as gardening, walking the dog, decorating, going shopping, hoovering and doing house chores, cleaning the car etc. can all be included. Also going to the gym, swimming or any other sporting activities. These activities are routine and can be done almost without thinking, yet it keeps your mind gainfully occupied. Doing normal things is mentally reassuring that things are normal and as they should be, though, in reality, they are not. In the case of those activities in which you can have a goal, then you can give yourself the feeling of having achieved something. By being focused on accomplishing something should it be mowing the lawn or swimming twenty lengths of the swimming pool, this will automatically distract you from your grief. It will reward you with a sense of achievement.

First Aid in Bereavement

You also need to plan in a treat or two for yourself. You need treats which will lift your spirits. Nothing need be expensive just something which is a treat for you. Something you can look forward to as the day progresses. Only you will know what these are. They might include a bubble bath, buying fresh flowers (your favourites), watching a favourite DVD or a film, having your hair cut or styled, buying some chocolates, a visit to a coffee shop, a favourite meal (even if it is a McDonald's), listening to favourite music, going shopping at your favourite shop or shopping centre, or reading/getting lost in a book. It doesn't need to be anything significant. Your lost loved one would want you to have peace, happiness, fulfilment and joy, just as you would wish it for them should what has happened have been reversed. So, don't feel guilty about these little pleasures and treats or sharing laughter and fun. These give you something to look forward. It occupies your mind and leaves no space for grief to fill. These plans are no guarantees that grief will not ambush you but being organised against it and gainfully occupied does help. Being active, mentally and physically; whatever you are doing is also in itself an excellent antidote to grief.

On some anniversaries, you might be able to help someone, for serving others lightens your burden. It would include helping someone with a problem at work or helping someone by doing their shopping. Or by prior arrangement helping someone with their gardening or tidying up. Feeling wanted and needed is great for blowing away sadness and grief.

If you feel strong enough, or that it will be especially helpful, then it is perfectly okay to set aside quiet time, in a calm place, and there reflect with gratitude on what your loved one meant to you and particularly in connection with that specific anniversary. You also need time to reflect and time alone so that you can face the pain of your grief, which will help the healing process. The quiet place could be somewhere in your garden, your bedroom, or other room in the house. If you wish you can thank God in prayer for all that your loved one did in their life and did for you and meant for you. Or you can mentally just thank your loved one for these things. During this time, you need to think of your loved one, and the times you spent with them. The message to your loved one within these memories should be I loved you and I always will. Your ultimate aim is to let these memories fill you with gratitude and thankfulness. Only participate in this as you feel strong enough to do so. You also may need a quiet time to pray, read a favourite Bible passage or poem. Then quietly reflect on the past and your journey through grief so far and perhaps what your hopes are for the future. Take this opportunity to think through what the next year or two or even five years, may have in store for you. Doing this with your loved one in your thoughts helps you to get things into perspective and to carry the influence and memories of your loved one into your new life. Make sure you are comfortable and just relax giving yourself a set time maybe 10 minutes (half an hour at the maximum) before you return to undertake your next planned activities. If you feel strong enough to do this then as the day progresses, don't be afraid, when grief encroaches, to say to that grief go away. I will meet you in my quiet time at 4.00 pm (or whatever time you have set) that grief will be your time. Plan something to do at the end of the 10 minutes so that you place a limit on this time.

On one or more anniversaries which are particularly special for you, then if you feel strong enough, and that it would help, you may wish to visit the grave of your loved one. You may wish to take flowers or a flower which had a special meaning for you both. Spend some time at the graveside and/or in the quiet surrounds of the cemetery or the crematorium. Use this time in the same way as you would use the quiet time outlined above. If it is a lonely place, then consider asking someone to go with you who can wait in the car where they will be in visual contact with you.

It is, however, a good idea to avoid activities which have been undertaken with your loved one on previous anniversaries. For example, should the anniversary involve a celebratory meal, avoid the restaurants which would recall the anniversary shared there with your loved one. By all means, have a celebratory meal if you wish, but have it, not alone, but somewhere completely different and with friends or close family. This may be the case, for example, on your birthday.

An alternative way to fully occupy the day of the anniversary is to plan an away day. Treat yourself to an away day visiting a nearby town or city for the day. There you can fully occupy yourself visiting the shops or taking a meal out. Maybe also include a visit to the cinema or a theatre or other place of interest if you can interest a trusted friend to accompany you so much the better. The place to be visited should not hold any special memories of your loved one. Perhaps on later anniversaries, you may feel strong enough to visit such sites, when you know that such a visit will bring back nostalgic memories which will be recalled with gratitude and happiness.

Christmas, especially the first one without your loved one, also needs careful thought and planning if you are not to leave yourself wide open to grief. Something different is the safest approach and celebrate it not alone but with friends and/or family. If you usually celebrate Christmas at your home with your close family then think about celebrating it at your son or daughter's house. If this is not possible, then consider taking your close family out for Christmas dinner at a local restaurant. Alternatively, stay at a hotel over the Christmas period should this be financially possible. Another possibility is to take a family holiday perhaps abroad over Christmas. If you are going to be on your own at Christmas then certainly consider booking into one of the many establishments which offer you accommodation and a Christmas celebration with other guests.

Continuing to go on holidays and undertaking other leisure time activities are a valuable aid in recharging our batteries, building a new life and coming to terms with our grief. The fear of being ambushed by grief may lead to an avoidance of going on holiday or other similar activities. The possibility of such ambushes can be mitigated by careful planning, which should include the following. Plan these activities so that you do not go alone but go with a friend(s) or relative(s). Plan them to avoid the places, at least initially, which will be full of memories of being there, with your loved one. If you enjoyed visiting the theatre together, then go with an arranged party or with a friend(s). Go on holidays with relatives or friends. Thus, you will not miss out on these activities which bring you enjoyment and which enable you to recharge your emotional, mental and physical batteries, which you must do. In these ways, you will minimise the occasions when grief can ambush you. You will be bringing enjoyment into your life, which is what your loved one would have wanted for you, as you would have wished for them should the roles have been reversed.

As time passes by there is no way to avoid those special dates and occasions or the emotions they inevitably bring. The best way to manage them is to plan for them. You need to plan what you are going to do and vary this between time spent alone and time spent with other people, between time spent doing things and time spent reflecting. As the anniversaries pass, you will become increasingly aware of which activities are of most benefit to you. It will

# First Aid in Bereavement

help you to plan which activities to undertake and how much time to spend on each of these activities.

An upcoming anniversary has already been compared with a coming exam. The day of the exam will come, that is out of your control. The day of the anniversary will also in like manner come for it is also out of your control. What you can do in preparation for those days is to control what you can control. In the case of an exam, revise and prepare for it thoroughly. In the case of an anniversary plan activities to fully occupy you on that day. Take control of what you can control. It is the essence of tackling any difficult situation, be it in grief or any other area of your life.

Be realistic; you will inevitably feel sad on the occasion of anniversaries. Still, you can and must fight back against grief. You do not have to sit there and let grief use you just like a punching bag. It is not what your lost loved one would have wanted for you. Plan your day to minimise grief's opportunities. Put yourself first. Remember to be kind to yourself at all times. Yes, it is OK to cry, and if necessary, you must allow yourself the time to cry. Do not be put off doing things with friends because you might cry. If you are with others and you feel tears coming on, excuse yourself "to powder your nose". Then go somewhere suitable to cry, the toilet, for example, before re-gathering yourself and returning. Feel entirely justified to explain that you have just been ambushed by grief because today is the anniversary of ..........

# 14 WHAT TO DO ABOUT HELPING SOMEONE ON THEIR JOURNEY THROUGH GRIEF

**A useful reservoir of ideas to be used in first aid for friends and relatives to help and support others on their journey through grief.**

In our 21st century society, there are many social pressures which are applied through advertising, fashions, celebrities and public opinion which are aimed at guiding and determining our thoughts and actions. We are pressurised by advertisers and the leaders of public opinion in many ways, including what we should wear, what we should buy, how we should behave, to what we should aspire. One notable exception to all this is found when we come to death and grief. In these situations, there are no generally accepted guidelines as to how we should respond. There follow some practical suggestions on how help and support can be given to those who have lost a loved one. Beginning with what to do at the time of the death and extending into the journey through grief.

Well over a century ago, in Victorian times, mourning was a public way of life. Everyone knew what to do and how to do it. There is no such common approach in today's society as to how to behave when faced by the death of a loved one or someone who is mourning the death of a loved one. The Victorians, like the ancient Egyptians, had elaborate rituals concerning death and grief. Mourning was a very public ritual and customs determined how people should behave. These Victorian rituals referred mainly to women. Though men were required to wear black, it was for a lesser time, and they had more freedom to choose for how long they mourned. It reflected the fact that men must

# First Aid in Bereavement

continue with their daily work routine. The death of a spouse required the most extended period of mourning this lasted two years for a widow. She would be clad in black crêpe and wear a veil over her face for the first year of mourning her spouse. This was full or deep mourning. It was followed by a year of half-mourning during which the widow could throwback her veil to reveal her face and replace her black crêpe dress with a black silk dress. During the last six months of these two years, dresses could be worn incorporating other suitable colours such as purples and lilacs. Unassuming jewellery, such as black jet, could also now be worn.

During full mourning, the only social functions a widow could attend were those relating to the church. The mourning period for other deceased relatives was less. Parents mourning a child and a child grieving for parents were expected to be in full mourning for nine months and half-mourning for a further three months. For a sibling, this became three months of full mourning followed by three months of half-mourning. In the case of other relatives, such as aunts and cousins and in-laws, public mourning ranged from six weeks to 3 months. The mourning dress of men required a black suit and black armbands. Even babies would wear their white baby clothes with black borders, and white handkerchiefs would also have a black border.

The production and sale of mourning clothes were big business for clothiers. To save costs, people would dye their regular clothes black and then bleach and re-dye them following the period of mourning. People who did not follow these customs faced being ostracised. People did not visit the bereaved person until they had made an appearance at church which might be a week or ten days after the funeral. The wearing of these mourning clothes publicly indicated to everyone that the person was enduring a period of sadness and melancholy, and people knew to treat them accordingly. It was not unusual for children to see their mother dressed in black for almost the whole of their childhood. Their mother would have been in mourning for one relative or another, including her children. During Victorian times 15% of children died by the age of 5 with many also dying in later childhood. For those who survived life expectancy rose from 38 in the 1830s, at the beginning of Queen Victoria's reign, to 48 in 1901 at the end of her reign. Today we may be thankful that such restrictive customs do not persist. However, this does leave us with no social guidance as to how to mourn and no provision of an outward sign that someone may be grieving and need support or help or sympathy. The various Victorian time limits for mourning, give us a useful guide as to how long we may experience our more profound feelings of grief and therefore the length of time that may be needed in coming to terms with that grief. In the 21$^{st}$ century, with no outward signs through the clothes which we wear, we may be unaware of the grief being experienced by an acquaintance. It can often be the case nowadays, with families being spread so far apart. We may be unaware of the death of someone's cousin or an even closer relative. The death of someone's parents or a sibling may be unknown to us if the deceased is living 100 or 200miles away or even in another country, especially if the person who has been bereaved has not been met recently.

The following will give some guidance in providing help and support to people who are grieving. **The role of the supporter is primarily just to be there**. To be there and to listen patiently and perceptively. The nature of the help you can offer will depend on the time, which has elapsed since the death. It will also rest on how the bereaved person is coping with their journey through grief. We will begin with suggestions on how to help, commencing with the time immediately after the death. These are general suggestions and may be modified, in the light of the particular circumstances of the loss, especially if these have been traumatic or difficult.

On hearing of the death do get in contact with the bereaved friend or relative. This may take several forms. All will depend on the closeness of the relationship and your personal feelings. Every one of the following is appropriate. If the relative or a close friend are living nearby, you may wish to visit. It may be best to telephone first to arrange a suitable time because of all the other arrangements which have to be made in the immediate aftermath of a death. Other forms of contact include writing a letter, sending a sympathy card, telephoning, sending an e-mail and sending a text message so long as its content can be appropriate and long enough not to appear abrupt. These messages and the purpose of a personal visit should be to offer your sympathy and concern. If possible, it is also valuable to share an anecdote, a memory of something you did with the deceased or some of the qualities or activities which you admired or valued in the deceased. In such messages be prepared to mention the deceased by name. It will provide reassurance that the deceased person is not forgotten and this will be of comfort to the bereaved person. Such written messages will be much valued and are a lasting testimony which can be and will be read and re-read over the coming months and years. They will be a continuing help in that person's journey through grief.

The most valuable help is that of a practical kind. It is perhaps best offered in conversation either on a visit or on the phone when something definite and beneficial can be directly arranged. Particular circumstances will tailor the form of this help, don't offer to cut the lawn if there is no lawn to mow. That is unless you can carry off such a statement as a joke, which will be appreciated, and perhaps more so on these occasions when humour can bring some joy and normality into so much grief. In the immediate aftermath of a death practical help with meals both saves the time and the energy of the bereaved in preparing them. This time can be devoted to the many other things which need to be done. It might include going round to make the meals in the house; taking meals round either sandwiches, a meal already cooked in a slow cooker, or similar; or an invitation to come round for a meal or taking the mourner(s) out for a meal. Other practical help, also saving time and energy, can include washing clothes and ironing clothes (even taking them to the laundrette), cleaning the house, walking the dog, digging the garden, mowing the lawn, shopping or being in to answer the phone in those first few awkward hours following the death and of course your physical presence to support and be there for your friend in the days, weeks and months ahead.

The next major emotional event after the death is the funeral. Your presence at the funeral is important, but this will be governed by other things which will be understood. So, do not be afraid to explain why you cannot attend. This may be due to work commitments, holidays; perhaps you still feel too upset by a recent bereavement of your own to participate in a funeral risking being plunged into grief. These explanations will be fully understood. If you have been recently bereaved, then you will be seen as someone who is travelling on the same road. You will be welcomed and spoken with as someone who is also experiencing that journey through grief. If you can attend the reception after the funeral, then do so. That you are present will be seen as support by the bereaved person, and you will also be giving support to your fellow mourners. Being there is important even if you do not get the opportunity to speak to the person or people most affected by the death. Some funerals provide cards to be filled in so that those attending can be known.

# First Aid in Bereavement

Concerning what to say at funerals, the best advice here is to talk about and discuss the same topics you would should you be meeting the same people on a different more commonplace occasion. This will make up most of the conversation. It will help to reassure people and give them the feeling that things are as they always are even though they are not due to the circumstances of your meeting together. When meeting the chief mourners offer your condolences, speaking along the lines outlined in the letters mentioned earlier in this chapter. As in your messages do not be afraid to mention the deceased by name for, he/she will still be very real in their minds, and this will be a source of comfort to them. Such a mention will also demonstrate that you have not forgotten the deceased person, and this will be another reassurance.

**In initial meetings with the bereaved and subsequent meetings, all you need to concentrate on is physically being there and listening without making any judgements.** In the immediate aftermath of the death, your friend or relative may well wish to talk a great deal about the last few hours or minutes of the deceased's life. Just allow this to happen. Listen without comment. It is all part of the coming to terms with the death of the loved one. It is part of the whole process of healing. The value of this repetition is two-fold. First, it helps cathartically to enable the bereaved person to come to terms with and more fully understand and accept what has happened. Secondly, it helps the bereaved to dispel any lingering emotions of denial or disbelief for each rehearsal of the events is reinforcing the knowledge that the death did happen. Later this topic will lose its primacy and become mixed in with the other memories of the deceased person.

The whole listening process should be one of passive listening. Don't interject with "I know how you must be feeling" because you don't. Everyone's grief is unique to themselves. Don't attempt to give people solution's to the dilemmas and mixed emotions which have come with their grief, by saying things like, "Be strong". Or "Think of all the things you have to be thankful for". Or "We can all feel thankful she is out of pain and suffering now". Those who are grieving are aware of such things, but at present, they don't meet the immediate needs of their grieving so shortly after the death. At some time in the future, such statements may well meet these needs, and these and similar comments will be more appreciated. Later such comments will serve as a means of introducing the sharing of thoughts and memories of the deceased.

Let the person who is grieving lead the grieving. This means allowing them to feel free to cry and feel sorrow and hurt and to express those feelings in words and actions when we meet with them. Also do not seek to define how long the grieving should go on by statements such as, "It's now six months since Peter died you should be getting over all this by now". **The role of the supporter is primarily just to be there for the person who is grieving, to be there and to listen patiently and perceptively.**

Do not feel that you have to ask after the well-being of the person who has been bereaved every time you meet. This is especially so if they are attending a social or leisure time activity. It may be that they are feeling relieved to be doing something which enables them to take their minds off their grief. Your enquiries will only remind them of their grief which they were hoping to escape from for a while.

Everyone's grief is unique for there are many variable factors which play into the death which influence the grief being experienced. These include the age and previous experience of such losses for the mourner. How old the deceased was and whether the death was sudden or protracted. What was the relationship which the mourner had to the deceased and the closeness of that relationship? All these things and many more will affect the way a person grieves and for how long. This uniqueness of everyone's grief needs to be taken into account when help and support are being offered. As previously mentioned, the best advice is to let the mourner lead. Some mourners may be happiest just talking about their past memories in which case be a perceptive listener.

Particularly uncertain times for those who mourn are the anniversaries of events which were shared with their loved one. These include birthdays and other significant celebrations of which their wedding day will be the most poignant. There are also family celebrations such as Christmas. These occasions of a family get together inevitably highlight the missing person's absence as well as recalling happy times previously spent together with the loved one on these occasions. For this reason, these events need to be planned and carefully managed to minimise grief's impact. New emotional anniversaries will be created the most significant being the date the death, and the funeral. Dependent on the circumstances, other dates might be linked with the diagnosis of the fatal illness and the final admittance into the hospital. Other celebrations such as other people's weddings, will also be trying and a stark reminder of the loss should that loss be a spouse. Attending someone else's funeral, especially a short while after the death can also be a difficult time. The supporter needs to be aware of all these events. This is especially so in the case of a birthday or a wedding anniversary, which occurs shortly after the death. It is also beneficial for mourners to plan activities on anniversaries so that they are occupied and focused on a variety of things to do (see the chapter on 'What to do about Anniversaries'). Their minds are therefore occupied and are not easy prey, to being ambushed by grief.

Further, these activities lay down new memories which dilute the old memories and so make future anniversaries less poignant. Go along therefor with their plans and support the grieving person in planning for these anniversaries. Similarly, with Christmas and other family occasions, if you have a part to play in these, discuss with the mourner the possibility of doing something different, particularly on the first and second anniversaries. It will again lay down new memories which will dilute the old memories. It will decrease the opportunities for grief to ambush the mourner on these occasions when familiar activities recall memories of doing them with their lost loved one.

In the case of anniversaries, the best help you can offer is to work with the mourner in planning activities. The types of suitable activities are listed in the chapter on 'What to do on Anniversaries.' Encourage the mourner and support them in undertaking these activities, joining in wherever this is helpful or necessary. Of these activities, some will appeal more to women than too men and vice versa. These include; taking them to and sharing in a pampering session at a beauty salon; buying and booking them into such a pampering session; arranging to take them to a sporting event; inviting them to take part in a sporting event such as a game of golf; asking them out for a meal or to attend the theatre. It may well be that you can invite the mourner to help you with some task or activity. By all means, do this for being able to help someone else is a sure way of lightening the burden for the mourner. Giving help to someone else helps to wash away the sadness in the life of the mourner. These activities can also be undertaken at other times. Should the mourner require some time alone then do what you can to facilitate this. It might be driving them to a place in the countryside which played a particular part in that anniversary or their life with their loved one. There you can keep a safe eye on the mourner in what might be a

# First Aid in Bereavement

lonely spot, while they spend some time alone with their thoughts and memories.

Similarly, be prepared to help the bereaved person to do something different at Christmas, perhaps go away with them for Christmas to a hotel or assist them to do this. Or encourage the mourner to spend Christmas at home if relatives were always visited or visit relatives if Christmas was always celebrated at home. In this way, new memories will be formed to dilute the old memories, as well as limiting the opportunities for grief to ambush the mourner. Be prepared to fit in with the plans of the mourner, or be ready to suggest to the mourner plans along these lines. In all of this common sense will be needed as will sensitivity to the particular mourner's needs and interests.

There will be times when your friend or relative needs a quiet time in which to grieve and cry, be prepared for these occasions for they are a necessary part of the healing process. Also, there will be times when your friend or relative will be ambushed by grief. You need to be prepared for these occasions and allow the tears to fall while being there for your friend or relative.

As for the length of time that these more profound effects of mourning are felt, this will vary from person to person depending on the nature and the depth of the relationship with the deceased. A rough guideline can be taken from the Victorian examples, thus for a spouse two years, for a parent one year. These may extend for much longer, perhaps a decade or more for some. The feelings of grief will remain with the mourner for the rest of their lives while diminishing in intensity as the years pass.

There are no national figures or statistics, but many people estimate that some 10% -20% of people undergo bereavement counselling in some shape or form and for some people bereavement therapy. This is mainly necessary where the death has been particularly tragic or sudden, or where there have been other emotional factors involved. Should you feel your friend would benefit from this, then such help can be sought through a doctor or organisations such as Cruse Bereavement Counselling. The vast majority of people have an inbuilt resolve and ability to undertake their painful and challenging journey through grief and to emerge successfully at the other side. Friends and relatives have a part to play in helping with this journey.

In general terms, you must be there for your friend or relative over the coming months and even years. You must be prepared to be a ready listener and someone to whom they can turn for support with confidence and assurance. Along the journey, there may well be setbacks when grief once again breaks into the mourner's life for, we never lose our memories of loved ones. As time goes by, these will be interspersed with longer and longer periods when life can be seen to be returning or has returned to normality. In these situations, when grief returns the support required will be broadly along the lines described above. As the bereaved person begins to rebuild their new life, your help and support will be much appreciated to enable this to happen. It may take the form of encouraging the bereaved person to join a new group or take up a new activity. It will broaden and develop their new life and so build-up new memories with new friends and acquaintances. It may also be necessary to be actively involved in this. You may need to join in new interests and new organisations with your friend or relative to provide support and help along the way. Your support and encouragement will be required to ensure that your friend maintains contact and social interaction with old friends, acquaintances and activities. For in so doing, they will remain in contact with relatives and old friends who are best able to provide the help and support needed on the journey through grief. The journey through

## First Aid in Bereavement

grief will continue for the rest of your friend's or relative's life, and you must be prepared to journey with them as long as you are needed.

A word of caution needs to be made here. Supporting someone on their journey through grief will take its toll on you, emotionally, mentally and even physically. Only involve yourself to the extent that you know you will be able to cope. You must avoid becoming overwhelmed or debilitated by being caught up in your friend's grief so that you become an emotional casualty of grief yourself. If you feel this happening then reduce your commitment and involvement, if necessary, explaining why, and seek to draw other friends or relatives in to share the burden or take over from you. Should you feel that your friend is not coping on their journey through grief (see the chapters on 'Normal Signs that you are coping with Grief' and 'Signs that you are struggling to cope with Grief'). It will be necessary, ensure that professional help is sought through a doctor or counsellor.

In whatever situation you are in life then verbal encouragement and support for someone have a vital part to play. It is also the case in grief. Bereavement is one of the most sensitive and emotionally charged situations in life. We should not leave ourselves entirely at the mercy of grief. We can take steps to mitigate its effect through verbal encouragement and support of one another.

Encouragement is essential by telling someone who is bereaved that they have done something well or have achieved something.

Do not be afraid to congratulate someone who is grieving. It might be as a result of sorting out banking arrangements. It might be in connection with solving a particular problem. It might be in getting the plumber to mend a leak.

Thus, we might say "You've done tremendously well in getting all those banking arrangements sorted out so quickly." Or, "Getting those three quotes and a plumber to fix that leak couldn't have been done better". In mourning, such comments not only help in the usual way in which praise does. They are also a boost, through informing the person who has been bereaved how well they are coping on their journey through grief.

People can also be encouraged by telling them that they are doing the right things to help them on their journey through grief. For example, when they are going out and socialising as they usually would have done or are planning for the future, for instance, a holiday. In such situations, you could encourage by saying for example; "You are doing just the right thing."

When the bereaved person goes out with their friends or has a friend to stay, you could say, "I am pleased that you are meeting people, it will be a great help to you."

Do not be slow to praise other situations in which the bereaved person has had success, for example, achievement at work. When the bereaved person says they have done or achieved such and such at work you could say; "Well done! You are coping very well with the challenges of work. That is great you are making good progress on your journey through grief." Or, words to that effect.

It will be helpful to encourage the bereaved person generally. Tell them that you are very proud of the way they are coping with the demands of work, or travelling to the office, or fitting in social and leisure activities all alongside work and/or caring for their family. Such statements also indicate to the bereaved person that they are coping very well with their grief and that things are working out for them. It gives them encouragement and confidence in facing the future.

The aim is to encourage and reassure the mourner that they are doing the right things and travelling in the right direction. It, in turn, will help them to aim at doing more of the same or similar things. Like everyone who has experienced the shock of bereavement, they will feel that they are blundering around in a thick fog. Unsure of which way to go and not knowing whether or not they are just going around in circles. This kind of encouragement will reassure them that they are travelling in the right direction to come out of the fog and not stay in it going around in circles.

Following the death of a loved one, some people are worried about the prospect of responding to people's inquiries about the death of their loved one. For many people following a recent bereavement, simple everyday questions and conversations can become emotionally charged. Simple questions like "How are you?" come with a whole host of emotional overtones when addressed to someone who has been recently bereaved. These worries can be alleviated by rehearsing such questions and suitable answers with the mourner. Or if you are the mourner rehearse them to yourself or with somebody you trust. Some examples are as follows;

"How are you?" (Answer: "I am OK, thank you.")

Or " How are you feeling?" (Answer: " I am feeling fine. I am over the shock of (name of the person who has died) death, and I am getting on with my life again.").

Or "Do you think about (name of the person who has died) a lot?"

(Answer: "Yes. I sometimes think about him/her, and it makes me feel sad, but I am managing OK")

Or "I was sorry to learn of the sudden death of (name of the person who has died)". To which an answer might be "Thank you. It was a shock, but I am getting over it." "Getting over it" might not be entirely accurate. Still, it does reassure people and defuse the necessity for them to ask you further questions.

There are no right or wrong answers to such well-meaning inquiries. The main issue is that the mourner should feel comfortable with the answer they give. Should they wish to provide a more detailed fuller response, then that is perfectly acceptable though usually, the inquirer is not seeking such a response.

If the person who is grieving is "armed" with suitable answers, having already rehearsed them. They will be more confident going into social settings and less deterred from doing so. The bereaved person doesn't have to tell the truth, the whole truth and nothing but the truth, just an answer which they are comfortable with giving. After all, the person asking the question would be stunned if the mourner took a couple of hours to "truthfully pour out their heart to them" about how they felt. It is not what the person asking the question is expecting. Though if you are speaking to someone whom you trust it can be helpful for you, to give a fuller more detailed answer as to how you feel.

Should a person move into a new social setting where people may well not know of the recent bereavement, for example, a new job or a new area in which to live. Then innocent questions can become emotionally loaded. Questions such as, "How is your husband?" Or "Where are you going on holiday this year?" Such issues, which are generally harmless conversation pieces, will, following on from the recent death of a loved one, almost inevitably result in the mourner being ambushed by grief. Some rehearsal as to possible responses to such questions which are likely to be asked will therefore also be helpful. Should it be known that the mourner will be moving into a new social setting. Example responses to such innocent enquiries might be; "I hope you won't be shocked, but my husband/wife died seven weeks ago from cancer." Or "I didn't realise that you did not know that my husband/wife died six months ago from a heart attack."

To avoid such situations arising it is as well to inform places of work and social groups which have been attended by the mourner. Also, ensure that the funeral director informs people of the bereavement through local newspapers. He is the ideal person to advise on how best to do this as he will be aware of the local situation.

If you can help the bereaved person with some strategies to use and example answers to give in these situations, then this will be a big boost in confidence for them. Such discussions also provide a meaningful opportunity to help the person come to terms with their grief and to ask any questions of you, which may be troubling them. It also provides the mourner with an opportunity to release their emotions by talking to you about the death and how they are feeling.

All of this will boost confidence and help the resumption of a normal lifestyle of meeting and being with friends and family. Thus for the mourner life goes on as before their loss. These are the people best-placed to provide help and support on the journey through grief. If the fear of such conversations become a deterrent from meeting people, the mourner may remain isolated, possibly reluctant to even leave their home. To help overcome this, the rehearsal of possible answers to such questions with a trusted friend or relative can be a big help.

Rehearsing and discussing such scenarios is also an ideal opening to discuss the death. It will provide an opportunity for the bereaved person to share their emotions. Thus, enabling you to assess how well they are coping with their grief, as well as providing you with the opportunity to provide help, support and advice, where and if necessary. Also bear in mind whether you feel "strong enough" to deal with some of these topics before going into them with the bereaved person.

The aim is to give the mourner help to be able to go out and face the world. By doing this, they can once more take control of their life and enable it to return to being as healthy as it can be in the circumstances. Should you be the person who has lost their loved one, then you may find that rehearsing the answers to these questions will help you on your journey through grief. Rehearse them on your own or with a trusted friend or relative.

Another situation which can cause embarrassment is as follows. A recently bereaved person may find people being apologetic or covered in confusion when they suddenly realise that the bereaved person is there and they have been talking for example about death or cancer or another fatal illness. A suitable response might be "You don't need to apologise, I am quite alright talking about these things." Or "It's OK we all need to talk about such things." In truth, the mourner may not feel like this. Still, such statements take the tension out of the situation and allow regular social intercourse to resume and proceed.

Someone can be helped on their journey through grief by pointing out to them that they are making good progress and that life is going on as usual. This can be done by reminding them of the good things which are happening in their lives. It can be done by questioning them about some of the things which have been happening to them. How long, following a bereavement, to begin doing this is a matter of judgement. It should not be undertaken should it cause any distress or upset, either to the bereaved person or oneself. In avoiding such upset, it may be beneficial to allow six months or more to elapse since the death before using this strategy. It will allow a reasonable amount of time to have passed since the loss allowing time for some good things to have happened in that time. It could be tried sooner if it was felt to be beneficial to the mourner.

The purpose of these questions is to enable the mourner to realise that they are doing the normal things they would have been doing in life before their loss and also gaining benefit from doing them. Having realised this, then the mourner is given more confidence to plan their lives and to take on board these beneficial events and activities and repeat them. Questions like "What is the best thing which has happened to you this past week?" Or "What is the best thing that you have done this past month?" Or "What did you enjoy doing most today?" It is aimed at making the person who has been bereaved realise and appreciate that "good things" are going on in their life. Things which they will want to do again and which they have found beneficial and gained enjoyment from doing. It is helping them to realise that their new life is not all sadness and gloom. Other helpful questions to ask include; "What things were you doing when you felt the most peaceful during this past week?" Or "What things were you doing when you were feeling the calmest this past month?" It is a way of getting the bereaved person to see and realise that there are times when they do feel calm and peaceful. It also flags up for them that they can repeat these activities or situations to achieve peace and calm again. "What made you laugh this past week?" "What was the funniest thing you experienced in the past month?" These questions open the eyes of the mourner to the fact that good things are happening in their life. It reveals that they are beginning to find enjoyment in life once again. As for the time scale to look back over, you can vary this; today or this week/ weekend or this month, or this past three months or even last year. Should you also be affected by the loss. If you wish, you could respond by also telling your answers to the above questions to the bereaved person. In this way, open up other activities for them to consider trying as well. You will also be letting the other person know that it is OK to enjoy life again and to look for what brings happiness, calm, peace and contentment. Should you be the one who has lost a loved one, with the same reasons in mind, you can ask and answer these questions of yourself. As the bereaved person answers these questions, they will realise that things are changing. They are moving on in their journey through grief. Their life is returning to a new normal.

A good time to introduce this approach might be at a quiet time, for example, after an evening meal. Or maybe Saturday or Sunday afternoon when you and the mourner have both got some energy left in your batteries. Maybe just look at one question "What was the best thing you have done this week?" or "What was the best thing which happened to you this week?" and explore this—perhaps also sharing your best thing. If it takes off, look at other questions. Later you might find it becomes a regular once a week (or more frequent) activity which you do regularly. If the bereaved person is not ready for this and does not wish to respond to these questions, then put it on one side for a later time on their journey through grief. Only try this approach if you think it will help. Do not take on this activity if you think it will seriously increase your stress levels or that you will not be able to cope emotionally.

# First Aid in Bereavement

This approach works equally well when occasions for its use arise naturally. For example, if the bereaved person says "I enjoyed doing ………………………….." It provides an opportunity to enquire "What other things have you enjoyed doing?" Thus, the bereaved person can be encouraged to see that good things are happening in their new life without their loved one.

The other side of this approach can be that the answers given may reveal that little if any progress is being made on the journey through grief. For example, if the mourner declares that nothing good has happened to them or nothing made them laugh or feel happy. Perhaps even going so far as to proclaim that nothing will ever happen to make them feel this way again because their loss has made them so sad. There will be occasions when many mourners think this way from time to time. Should these feelings persist or become the norm. Or should these be your feelings when you ask yourself these questions. It would indicate that help from a doctor or counsellor needs to be sought.

It is advisable to stick very much to the positives. At this stage, don't enquire into negatives by asking questions such as; "What made you feel sad this week?" Or "What was the worst thing which has happened to you today?" They have a value at the right time, by alerting people to avoiding such situations to prevent this sadness from happening again. Such questions can also be deliberately asked to open the door to talk about what makes the person feel sad and the causes for this. It brings the sadness out into the open so that it can be dealt with. It is a much more difficult task dealing with these negative feelings than dealing with positive emotions. If you are the person who has lost a loved one, you can ask and answer for oneself such negative questions. Again, only adopt this approach if you feel able to cope with the possible emotional responses and consequences.

People on their journey through grief can be helped by talking to other people in a similar situation. Meeting up with someone who is also grieving provides an immediate point of contact and source of empathy. Such conversations and meetings can be mutually beneficial. So, arrange for your grieving friend or relative to meet up with a mutual friend who has experienced grief. Alternatively, through the Bereavement Counselling Service, it is possible to join such people in bereavement groups. Also, some areas have a local widows group which meets regularly and will be on the look-out for new members. Local widower groups are almost non-existent, but widows groups are often happy to admit widowers.

Do not be reluctant to raise any practical issues or worries which you feel may be of concern to the person who has lost their loved one. They may be too caught up in their grief to have given them any thought. Raising these issues provides the ideal opportunity to bring them out into the open so that they can be dealt with and professional help sort if necessary. It enables such matters to be handled before they become a significant problem. It can be done through simple inquires such as; "How are you going to manage the garden now?" Should there be a large garden. Or "Can you afford to continue living the same lifestyle?" Should you have any concerns for the financial situation of the mourner mainly if it is the breadwinner who has died.

From the above, it can be seen that we are not totally at the mercy of grief. We can take steps to mitigate its effect through the support and encouragement of one another. All of this will be of help in a person's journey through grief. It will help them to cope with their grief as well as reassuring them that they are making good progress and that others are there to help. In undertaking these activities, it must be remembered that not all will be appropriate in all situations for each person's reaction to grief will be

First Aid in Bereavement

different. With this in mind temper, what is attempted to the individual responses of the bereaved person. Above all, allow the grieving person to take the lead.

# 15 WHAT TO DO ABOUT A NEW RELATIONSHIP

**Circumstances to be taken into consideration by a person seeking to decide on when, or if the situation is right, to form a new relationship with a new partner following the death of their spouse or partner.**

The following discussions primarily have remarriage in mind. It is because there is more statistical information available about remarriage. Many of the issues raised will equally apply in the case of civil partnerships or any other form of a long-term collaboration or relationship.

Whether to marry or form a long-term relationship is dependent on the age of the survivor. The older they are, the less likely they are to wish to create a new long-term relationship.

Many bereaved people successfully integrate the memories of the deceased loved one into their new life. It enables them to live their life as a single person with a new relationship with their deceased partner. It is based on memories which they carry into their new life and a love which transcends death.

Some, especially after a happy marriage, will prefer to live with their memories and use these to carry their loved one with them into their new life. Though their loved one is not physically present, they are present through the gift of memories. These can serve as a source of support as speculation is undertaken as to how the loved one would have reacted to the new life unfolding with its changed circumstances. You can still grow old with your lost love and in a sense, make new memories. It is always possible in your heart to feel the tie and the love which exists between you and your lost loved one. Saint Paul teaches us that love never ends (1Cor 13:8).

As you move into your new single life, there is no risk now of the heartache of affairs or new loves which might have split your partner or spouse away from you. You do not have to share your loved one with anyone except with those close to you as you discuss your memories of them together. You can now look forward to making the most of the opportunity to enjoy a single life with lots of friends. You can feel gratified to continue your new single life with your memories of your loved one.

Often the downside of taking on anew spouse or partner is overlooked. It will not be a like for like replacement of your first spouse or partner. There will be new idiosyncrasies and annoying habits to come to terms with. In the longer term, they will grow old, and you face the possibility of having to nurse a terminally ill person and face bereavement over again. There is the possibility that the new relationship will end in the heartache of divorce or a separation which might be acrimonious.

For some, the new life which begins following the death of a spouse or partner will at some stage involve a new spouse or long-term partner to replace the relationship which death has broken. There comes the point on the journey through grief when a widow or widower may consider a new partner. We shall consider here, factors which may affect such a decision as to whether to build such a new relationship or not as the case may be. These considerations will be similar to the ones operating when a person decides to remarry or take another long-term partner following divorce. Individual circumstances will significantly influence this decision, the major one being the age of the surviving spouse or partner. In the event of the death of a parent or a sibling, there is in many instances no question of such a replacement of the relationship being possible.

It is only over the past 20 or 25 years in bereavement counselling that people began to take seriously, the need to consider the issues surrounding making a new relationship with a new partner, in the counselling of people who have lost their spouse or partner. Previously it was as if counsellors were unaware of the fact that the close relationship with a partner, which might have lasted 5 or 50 years, had suddenly come to an end. No account was being taken of the fact that this close relationship, involving physical intimacy and sexual love within that marriage or partnership, had suddenly stopped. The resulting loss will have an impact both immediately in the bereaved person's life and on any similar future close relationships. In this chapter, we shall look at issues relating to the decision whether or not to build-up another close relationship with a new spouse or partner.

This situation, as we shall see, will be primarily governed by the age of the person concerned and their aspirations. As in all circumstances relating to grief, the situation will evolve in a unique way for each individual. For any given individual, it is not possible to predict with any certainty, whether or not a new relationship will be desirable. This is so because of the uniqueness of the personality of the mourner and all of the surrounding circumstances.

In the immediate aftermath of the death of a loved one, the emotional turmoil and grief are such that initially considerations of a marriage or a close relationship to replace the one which is passed are far from the mind of the grieving survivor. Grief is emotionally and physically draining. The libido is low as is self-esteem. There is no energy left to be wasted on dating and searching for a new partner.

New close relationships will not be a high priority with all the arrangements to be made, bills to be paid, and social and family upheaval following on from the death. It is perhaps fortunate that the search for another close relationship can be put off and the energy saved, to solve the many other more immediate problems. This searching will also be inhibited by the sudden swings in mood and the magnified ups and downs of life which the survivor will initially experience. There will come a time, perhaps after six months or a year or two or more, it will vary with individual people, when the survivor's thoughts turn to the possibility of finding a new partner. It is essential that the mourner feels emotionally healed and secure before they embark on seeking to remarry or establish a close relationship with someone. Failure to do this will almost inevitably lead to a failed new relationship or marriage.

The majority of statistics which do exist relating to this matter are for marriages as these have had to be legally recorded for centuries. In contrast, no such records are kept for other close relationships other than more recently for civil partnerships. We shall, therefore, speak of marriage, but these remarks apply equally well to civil partnerships and other close relationships. A significant influence when considering the issues of remarriage or a new intimate relationship will be the age of the bereaved person.

As with divorce, as a general rule, the younger the bereaved person is, the more likely they are to remarry. Also, there will be an age beyond which most people are not likely to want to remarry, though some people do remarry in their 70,s or 80's. Many of the people widowed in their twenties do remarry—some remarriages taking place in as shorter a time as one year since being bereaved. As a person's age passes beyond 35, then we would expect the frequency of people remarrying to decline. As the age at bereavement reaches 55 or more years old, then the majority will probably not remarry. In this context, when the age of the loss reaches 70, 80 or 90 years old, then such people are highly unlikely to be looking to remarry.

A bereaved person may well strike up a close relationship with another person but not get married. This might be to avoid financial disincentives, some of which are mentioned below. Such relationships, though they may be effectively a marriage in all but name, will not be recorded in any official statistics. Thus, as already mentioned a complete and reliable statistical picture of both remarriage and any new close relationships formed by the surviving spouse or partner, are not available for statistical analysis.

Because of the following considerations, we would expect people aged under 35 years old who lose their spouse to be the age group who remarry the most. They would also do so more quickly as compared with people who have passed this age who lose their spouse or partner. In the case of younger people in their twenties, they are under more pressure to remarry or form a close relationship. Such influences would include the following. They would have more prospective partners available to choose from, for many in that age group would not yet have married and will be looking for a partner. They also would have an extra incentive, because of their age, to get married. Having just begun to appreciate the excitement and joys of marriage, then they would be predisposed to seek to return to this fulfilling situation again. Having been married for such a short time, then remarriage will be the most appropriate means of filling the loss in their lives. It would meet their emotional and physical needs through another loving and caring spouse or long-term partner. There may be additional pressures such as on a man left with young children. He may wish to remarry to provide a mother for them rather than remain a single-parent household. Thus, choosing to avoid the possible difficulties both for himself and the children in being a single parent. Similar pressures would also apply to a woman with young children who would look to benefit from a breadwinner and may choose not to be a one-parent family. For these reasons, we would expect people bereaved in their twenties to remarry sooner rather than later. On the other hand, by the time a person has reached the age of 55, and above then bereavement plunges them into a different situation. We would expect these older people to remarry or form close relationships less often than younger people who have been bereaved. The pressures affecting them, which might deter them from remarriage include the following. Older people are at a different stage of their lives. They have a different set of considerations which come into play than is the case with young people. In terms of the family commitments of someone aged 55+, their children in all probability are now grown up, and they will have left the family home. It removes the need of another spouse or partner to balance up and complete the family and avoid any difficulties which may arise from being a one-parent family. There is also no longer the expectation and pressure to marry which some, if not all, twenty something-year-olds would feel. Having been married for a considerable number of years, then the loss is different from that of recently wed individuals. There is not the same novelty and freshness to married life nor so many unfulfilled dreams. So the hole left in their life is not so immediate and raw though bereavement remains a crushing blow. There is therefore not the same need to remarry, to fill the hole left by the loss when married life is still new and fresh, as is the case with twenty something-year-olds. The pool of prospective partners is also different for 55+-year-olds. There is no longer a pool of young people waiting to be married or actively seeking a partner. Now, the pool of people of a similar age consists of, those who will have been married and currently are either widowed or divorced. For the majority of this age group will be already married or with a partner. This limits the numbers and the variety of choice from which to choose a new partner. Also, some of the now single people will wish to stay single.

In this age group, a different set of financial matters also need to be taken into consideration. The 55+-year-old widow(er) may have a comfortable pension from her husband's/wife's/partner's employment and may lose this should they remarry. It is the case with some public sector workers pensions, and this extends to other types of work. It can result in people living in extremely close relationships with one another short of remarriage, to preserve such financial benefits. Other economic issues can also influence such decisions such as inheritance laws and the wording of wills. Once remarried, then without a will, the wealth of the first spouse to die will pass into the survivor's family. The disposal of properties and the allotment of the proceeds can cause similar related problems of who will inherit what. The security of owning your own home plus emotional links to it can inhibit the rationalisation of dwellings. It can swing a decision against remarriage or cohabiting.

People who have been married for a considerable number of years may find that in time their loss brings benefits. They do not wish to give these up and so are less inclined to remarry or take a partner than younger people are. These benefits include the freedom to make choices entirely based on what they want to do. There is no recourse to compromise or trade-off against the wishes of a spouse or partner. There may be no wish whatsoever to return to a time of compromise and trade-off. It may be especially so if the surviving spouse may have negative experiences of this over several years, from their previous relationship. There is the discovery that you are a new person with new goals for your life which you wish to see through without having to make any adaptation to the wishes of another.

You have discovered new ways of dealing with your worries and anxieties enabling you to live life to the full. Now you have no wish to compromise this by taking on the concerns and anxieties of another. Also, people who lose their spouse after a long and happy marriage may choose not to remarry or form another close relationship. They are content with their memories and feelings following their first marriage. They may not want to run the risk of being plunged into such grief and pain, yet again should they grow equally close to this new spouse or partner, who may then also die. The new relationship may also end in the pain of divorce or separation. For these reasons we would expect to find fewer people remarrying when they reach 55 and beyond than is the case with younger people. The opportunities for remarrying are also different between older men and women. Statistically, men die before their wives. In the case of a woman, there will be a relative shortage of men. In the case of a man, there will be a relative surfeit of women to choose from in the older age groups. Thus, we would expect that in older age groups proportionately more men remarry than women.

Further men tend to marry younger women, but it is much rarer for a woman to marry a younger man. Women tend to be more gregarious in having a group of close female friends to supply support and provide companionship than do men. It results in men seeking this close support and friendship through remarriage or an intimate relationship, rather than having it in place already through a close circle of friends. These factors in the over fifties age group help in predicting that proportionately more widowed men will look to remarry than will widowed women in similar circumstances.

At whatever their age, some people who are bereaved, do remarry or form a close relationship of an intimate nature.

It is, therefore, appropriate to ask why people remarry or form a new long-term close relationship. For ease of expression, I will again use the word marriage. However, what is set out here applies to every type of long-term close relationship which might be entered into. The reasons can be grouped under three broad headings. These are:

1. to gain a handyman or to gain a woman to maintain the home;
2. to experience love, care and intimacy once again;
3. to once again give and receive sexual love within the context of a loving and caring relationship such as that of a marriage or civil partnership.

There is one other reason which might stand alone or be a driving force for any of these three, and that is the fear of loneliness, which we shall consider later.

The first reason is to gain a handyman or a woman to maintain the home. It can best be explained through the case of a man who may wish to remarry to have once again someone to cook, do the washing and maintain the home. In some cases, this may well extend to having a kind of trophy wife in the sense of someone to be a host and to accompany him, for example, to business functions. It is possibly the worst reason to wish to remarry. A better solution is to contact a local business which will supply someone to do the cleaning and washing on a purely contractual basis, with no emotional strings attached. It ensures that what needs doing gets done without any emotional entanglement with the resultant risk of falling out and other discordant stressful scenarios. The hired help also does not come with a ready-made family whom you might, or might not, get on with or whom you might not be able to stand. In the case of a woman, the handyman is married to provide someone to do the decorating and DIY about the house, to do the garden and run the finances. It may also extend to providing the financial resources for the relationship. For the same reasons, this is also not advised. Far better to get in the local plumber or joiner as required and whose bathroom routines and other unusual habits and idiosyncrasies will not be found out about nor will they have to be put up with 24/7, because he will only be around for a short time it takes to do the repair.

The second reason for seeking a new partner is to experience once again the love, care and intimacy of a loving relationship. This relationship is looking for the close companionship of a marriage partner without sexual intimacy. As human beings, we need to know that we are loved and cared for by someone. It begins in childhood when that someone is our parents. It continues into adult life when that someone becomes a spouse or partner. Following the death of that spouse or partner, there remains that need. We may no longer need the intimacy of sexual love.

Nevertheless, it is still good to have someone hold our hand; someone with whom we can share our deepest worries and fears, our dreams and aspirations. Someone to hold us tight and kiss us good night; someone in whose arms we can wake up in the morning, with all of this within a platonic relationship with no strings attached. Such a relationship, if by mutual agreement, will work, for it provides the companionship for which we long. Each partner receives the loving care and attention of the other. However, both partners need to be clear from the beginning that this is what each is searching for. It is all too easy for such a relationship to come with strings attached, the strings of one partner expecting sexual intimacy. It need not be a barrier if both partners are happy to allow their relationship to develop in this way. Or one is prepared to trade off sexual intimacy for the love, care and companionship received in return.

The third reason for seeking a new partner is to once more receive and give sexual love within the context of a loving and caring relationship, such as a marriage or civil partnership. It fulfils in its entirety the purposes and needs of these relationships. Such a relationship has every reason to succeed with the mutual fulfilment and happiness of the two parties involved just as, but in different ways, the first marriage, or civil partnership, now broken by death, succeeded.

If the widow/widower is actively seeking a new spouse, then they must clarify in their minds the relationship which they are looking for on the grounds set out above. Know yourself and what you are searching for, and what you are prepared to accept is sound advice. It is also essential that there is talk with any prospective spouses, as the relationship develops, to establish as soon as possible what each is looking for in that new relationship. It will avoid any future disappointments and prevent the wasting of each other's time. Particularly with older people, for time and age matter in the successful search for a new spouse or partner. It is of course, entirely feasible that the fairy-tale love, at first sight, will prevail. However, it is more likely to be the prosaic horses for courses. The better you know your horse, both yourself and your prospective partner, the more likely you are to be suited to the course. Should you be seeking a long-term partner and not a marriage, all the above will still apply, if the relationship is to be mutually successful and beneficial.

As already mentioned, the fear of loneliness may be an additional driving force for any of the above three and for some, the sole reason for needing to seek a close relationship or marriage. Loneliness should not be a reason to seek to develop a long-term relationship. It will, in the long run, be far less trouble to get involved with a club, or group of like-minded people. It will provide the opportunity of building up several close friendships with many and varied people. It is preferable to seeking to establish a single relationship with someone with whom you may find that you are unsuited. This single relationship, should it fail, runs a serious risk of leaving you even more lonely than before. Friendship with several people neatly avoids this risk. Learn to enjoy your own company and get involved in doing the things you like to do. Friendships will follow, and your loneliness will never materialise. Keeping your old friends will also help to prevent loneliness. Whereas actively going about seeking a new partner, if done in the wrong way (e.g. the new partner being someone's erstwhile husband/wife) may alienate some, if not all, of your old mutual friends.

There is the issue of where to look for someone with whom to form any of the above relationships. The best place to start is with eligible people you know already. You already know them and therefore will already have a feel for their suitability for whatever type of relationship you envisage. Knowing them already will make it easier to discuss your aspirations and so establish how you see the relationship with that person developing further. There are others with whom you will have to clarify your relationship with if you wish to remain on the same friendly terms as in the past when you were married. For you will have no wish for your relationship with them to develop further or deepen in another direction. You should ensure that, if necessary, this is made clear to such people to avoid any future misunderstandings and possible hurt. In casting the net further afield the very best place to start is in joining one or more societies or clubs connected with your interests and where, in the case of a woman looking for a man, men are to be found. Not, therefore, predominantly or solely women-only organisations. These, however, will have a value in widening the base of the women whom you know who can provide help, support and companionship.

These clubs and societies will offer the opportunity to meet men in the flesh as it were, and you will have more chance of seeing them warts and all. You will also glean something of their background, married, divorced, a flirt or whatever. In the case of a man, clubs and groups should be joined where women make up a significant proportion of the membership.

Internet dating sites have sprung up and have provided an opportunity for people to meet and in some cases, provide the opportunity for more lasting relationships and marriage. However, you cannot see with whom you are dealing and run the risk of being disappointed and hurt. Knowing someone personally reduces many of these risks. For example, at a later date finding that the person is married with three children and has no intention to leave his/her family for you. Despite what they may have said on the internet when pretending to be 40 years old and divorced. Or that he/she is not the good looking 50-year-old person in the photograph (a photograph which was taken many years earlier), instead they are 70 and far more wrinkled. Even on the telephone, much can be learnt from the expression in someone's voice when they speak to you. All of this is lost on the internet. The anonymity of such sites is an ideal place for the fraudsters to date you and dupe you. Or just simply string you along to have fun or gratify their egos at your emotional expense. Steer clear of these sites is the safest advice unless you are sufficiently hard-nosed to follow to the letter all the safeguards and precautions necessary.

We must also mention a small group of people who are, shortly after bereavement, drawn to engage in a sexual relationship or sometimes multiple short-lived relationships. Several needs and emotions may drive this. It may simply be the need for another close relationship to plug the gap left by the loss of the spouse or partner. It may be an escape from grief. The prospect of a new sexual partner with all that this means in terms of time spent with a new partner, and the excitement and anticipation of this new sexual encounter can leave little time for grief. Thus, the hard work of grieving can conveniently and legitimately be put to one side, which may have consequences for that person's journey through grief at a later date. Other, more complex motives may drive it. It may be motivated by the need to gain revenge on the deceased by effectively being unfaithful to them. This revenge may be prompted by some action of the deceased in the past; perhaps they too were unfaithful. Or it may merely be a response to the death, where the lover is seen as having deserted them by dying and leaving them bereft and all alone. By dying the lover has pulled the plug on a comfortable situation. It provided for the sexual and emotional needs of the survivor. In revenge, the survivor seeks to regain at least some sexual fulfilment by taking another lover or lovers, thus getting back at the deceased spouse or partner. Or there may be other more complex and diverse personal driving forces at play.

On returning to the dating game, many people revert to how they were when last in this situation as a teen and twenty-year-olds before their marriage. They initially behave and feel emotionally as they once did as young people. Later they allow the maturity gained throughout the years of their marriage to influence their approach and attitude towards and with their potential new partner. It is understandable as their knowledge and experience of playing the dating game stem from that earlier time in their lives.

Before re-entering the dating game, you must take stock and are aware of your emotional and mental state so that you know that you are once more emotionally stable. If you allow your need to be loved and cared for to dominate you, you may act too hastily and precipitately and make wrong choices in your haste to be loved and cared for again. Also, there are some deceitful and sneaky people out there who will try to take advantage of you, especially when you are emotionally vulnerable. This having been said, when you feel emotionally strong enough, dating will open up new avenues in your life. A new relationship does not mean you are unfaithful to your deceased spouse or partner and you need not feel guilty. The contractual foundation of your marriage with your loved one was until death us do part, and sadly that has now happened. Should you find someone else with whom you wish to share the rest of your life, then that is happiness which you both should willingly embrace! You will carry your memories of your loved one into your new life with your new love, thus demonstrating that your new life is big enough for both loves. Bearing in mind also that your deceased spouse or partner would want you to be happy and cared for just as you would wish the same for them should the circumstances have been reversed!

Your close relatives and friends will take a keen interest in any budding or a prospective new relationship. Their reaction may vary from complete support and encouragement through to outright unmitigated opposition. If it is opposition in some form or other, then take the time to ask them why they feel opposed to your new relationship. It may be that they are struggling with their grief. The upheaval of the death of a loved one can leave some people yearning for stability. Your new relationship is another emotional upheaval on top of their struggle to come to terms with the emotional turmoil of the loss of a loved one. Or particularly in the case of children, both young and grown-up, having just lost one parent, they do not wish to lose another to a new partner as they struggle with their grief. It may be that they feel you are not yet over your grief and are seeking an escape route from heartache in the excitement of a new relationship. Alternatively, they may think that your new partner is taking emotional advantage of you and has ulterior motives which are to your detriment. Or they may feel that emotionally and personality-wise you are not a match for each other.

Take full heed to what they say for bereavement leaves us much more vulnerable to making wrong decisions, especially where emotions are involved. Bereavement colours how we see other people sometimes we see them more rosily than they are. Having listened to the thoughts of others, you must also realise that how the relationship continues is entirely in your hands. So, you have nothing to lose by listening to the opinions, for or against, of those who hold you, dear. It is the best way to avoid a new relationship which disintegrates into yet more heartache and emotional upset.

# 16 WHAT TO DO ABOUT MEMORIALS

**An explanation of how memorials can ease the burden of the loss of a loved one.**

The burden of our loss can be eased through memorials. Their value lies in helping us to adapt the memories of our lost loved one into our new life without their physical presence. Memorials enable us to encapsulate the 'essence' of what our loved one meant to us. This we can then carry into our new life. In one sense, it replaces the presence of our loved one. The memorial also provides us with a place where we can revisit our loved one through our memories whenever we choose. Throughout the planning of these memorials, our thoughts are directed to our loved one. Memorials will typically be planned to begin after the first few days or weeks following the loss. If you feel strong enough, they can be initiated immediately after the death. Some examples are set out below.

The gravestones in churchyards and cemeteries remind us of the need people feel now and have felt down the centuries of creating a lasting public memorial to a loved one who has died. Today, in an age of technology, as well as such memorials people establish other types of memorials. These might include one or more of the following.

1. Photograph Album - Selecting photographs depicting the life of the diseased including achievements and significant happenings, memorable family events and treasured memories, to be placed in a photograph album dedicated to the memory of a loved one.

2. DVD - Putting together a DVD made up of movie clips drawn from old cine film, old videos and more modern digital recordings. Perhaps with background music which was a particular favourite of a loved one.
3. Fund Raising - Carrying out a fundraising activity, for example, a sponsored cycle ride or a walk, and donating the money raised to an appropriate charity; for example, cancer research, should the person have died from cancer.
   This might be continued as such, in some shape or form, on an annual basis. In future years this could continue not specifically for fundraising but as a social event for friends and family. Some may wish to establish a standalone charity in the name of the deceased. Usually, this charity is linked in some way to the illness or other circumstances which caused the death.
4. Internet Website - Creating a website on Facebook or similar dedicated to the memory of a lost loved one.
5. Naming a Star - There are organisations which can be found on the web which will enable you to name a star after a loved one.

Included under this heading of memorials are the photographs of the loved one around the house. The planting of a tree or shrub in the garden as a quiet reminder of the deceased person.

Such activities have therapeutic benefits in helping to express our emotions while at the same time, acknowledging the value and meaning of the deceased person's life. They help us to make sense of the life and death of the person we loved. They help us to face up to and accept the reality of the death. They enable us to better integrate the memories of our loved one into our new life without their physical presence. Such activities also encourage and promote interpersonal support as we work with others on a sponsored event or with close family, for example, compiling a photograph album.

Our forebears in a pre-technological age meet these needs through erecting a gravestone and visiting a cemetery to tend a grave. These activities, even deciding the wording on a gravestone, help us to feel closer to the person who has died and so eases the burden of our grief.

As well as the public, outward memorials, to be shared with others, there are also private memorials which enable us to revisit our memories of our loved one. These might include visiting places of personal significance to ourselves and our loved one as well as the quiet recalling of treasured memories.

Included in these might be embarking on a journey or trip, especially if it is one with particular memories of being one undertaken with our loved one. It is repeated to honour and to recall the memory of our loved one.

These memorials are not a morbid revisiting of a lost past but are positive ways and means of helping to adjust to the future. They have the therapeutic benefits of helping to express our emotions and acknowledge the reality of the death of our loved one. They help us to cherish our memories, enlist the support of others and integrate the legacy of our loved one into our new life. They serve as a means of telling friends and family of the place we are at. They are a statement by the mourner that while fully acknowledging the death of a loved one. They are going to carry with them their memories of their loved one and integrate them into their new life. At a more personal level, they are a reminder that a person has fully acknowledged their loss. They also serve and help a person to integrate their memories into their new life for the years which they have left to live.

# 17 WHAT TO DO WHEN SOMEONE DIES

**Some useful contacts who will provide this information**

There is much to do in terms of administration and legal requirements when someone dies. It is advisable to ask a close friend or family member to assist you and to go with you to meet the various agencies which you will need to see. Your local authority Department for the Registration of Births and Deaths will provide you with a free booklet setting out your duties and obligations in the event of a death. If you know someone to be terminally ill, then it is advisable to obtain this booklet before their death. If the death is sudden, then your first opportunity to acquire this booklet maybe when you go to register the death. This booklet will also provide a checklist of what organisations you will need to contact, such as banks, pension offices, etc., as well as useful addresses such as undertakers. Such information can also be obtained from the internet should you wish to be forearmed before the death occurs. A good starting point is the government web site
https://www.gov.uk/after-a-death/overview.

# 18 WHAT TO DO ABOUT PROFESSIONAL HELP

### Some information on where to go to seek professional help

To find a local bereavement counselling service, you can look online. You can visit or contact your local GP practice, a church minister, local hospice or library or you may wish to contact your local Samaritans. The following are the national headquarters of some organisations set up to help bereaved people. Should they want advice or wish to talk about their feelings and the impact which the loss of a loved one has had on their lives. Your local GP Medical Centre is probably your best first port of call to seek professional help as they already know you and will in all probability be aware of the circumstances surrounding your loss. If necessary, they will be able to put you in touch with a bereavement counsellor, who may be attached to that Medical Practice.

Cruse Bereavement Care
Central Office
PO Box 800
Richmond
Surrey
TW9 1RG

National Helpline for bereavement support; Tel 0808 808 1677.

E-mail help for bereavement support;
helpline@cruse.org.uk

John N Greenwood

Age UK
Tavis House
1-6 Tavistock Square
London
WC1H 9NA

Advice line 0800 678 1602

Child Bereavement UK
Clare Charity Centre
Wycombe Road
Saunderton
Buckinghamshire
HP14 4BF

Support and Information; Tel 0800 02 888 40.

e-mail; support@childbereavementuk.org

Samaritans

Telephone number 116 123.

This number is free on any landline or mobile. It can be used any time 24 hours a day, 365 days a year.

Alternatively, ring or visit your local branch, details of which can be found on the internet.

e-mail; jo@samaritans.org

# PART 3 WHAT TO BELIEVE

# 19 THE MESSAGE OF JESUS

The message of Jesus is that God is our heavenly Father, and God has created everyone for eternal life. The Good News which Jesus proclaims is that everyone has a ticket for heaven, including our loved one.

There is a word association game which can be played whereby a famous person is associated with the reason for their fame. Thus, Isaac Newton will be followed by the answer gravity, Charles Darwin, with the answer evolution, Karl Marx, with the answer communism, but what of Jesus Christ. The answer which follows the name Jesus Christ is eternal life.

"What happens when we die?" Jesus' answer is, "You have eternal life." The message of Jesus is that God, our heavenly Father, has created everyone for eternal life. The ministry of Jesus was not about this life but eternal life. Jesus teaches us about God's heavenly kingdom. He reveals to us the many routes which lead there. Jesus also teaches us that God has provided an abundance of tickets for heaven. These tickets are available to all Christians and non-Christians.

Jesus declares that faith in him is all that is needed to secure eternal life. A study of these routes reveals that Jesus endorses three expressions of faith, the faith of the intellect, the faith of the emotions and the faith of actions. Jesus shows that the faith of actions is the faith that enables non-Christians and those who do not know of him to secure their place in God's heavenly kingdom, witness the Parable of the Good Samaritan (Lk10:25-37). The Good

Samaritan was a member of another religion, the Samaritan faith.

The one prayer which Jesus taught teaches that God is the heavenly Father of everybody. It is acknowledged by everyone who prays "Our Father who art in heaven."

The ministry of Jesus was all about the kingdom of God and the one prayer which Jesus taught, the Lord's Prayer, is also all about the kingdom of God.

The only line which does not refer to God's heavenly kingdom is often the one which catches our attention. "Give us this day our daily bread." Note for yourself how much this prayer is concerned with God's heavenly kingdom.

Our Father, who art in heaven,
hallowed be your name;
your kingdom come;
your will be done;
on earth as it is in heaven.
Give us this day our daily bread.
And forgive us our sins,
as we forgive those who sin against us.
And lead us not into temptation;
but deliver us from evil.
For yours is the kingdom,
the power and the glory,
for ever and ever.
Amen.

Line 1: This sets God our Father in his kingdom of heaven.

Line 2: The fact that God rules a heavenly kingdom, making him far more powerful and magnificent than any earthly king or kingdom, requires that we hallow or praise his name.

Line 3: This line longs explicitly for the coming of God's kingdom.

Lines 4-5: These lines also long for the kingdom, defining it as the place where God's will is done and longing for God's will to be done on earth with the teaching that where God's will is being done there is his kingdom.

Line 6: Refers to this world. But even so, this line can be interpreted as God giving us sustenance until the day we die and fully gain his heavenly kingdom.

Line 7-8: Getting into God's heavenly kingdom is dependent on forgiving others when they offend us. Jesus explains these two lines in the following verses in Matthews gospel (Mt 6:14,15). Jesus explains we are to forgive others; otherwise, God will not forgive us, and we will bar ourselves from God's heavenly kingdom because our sins will keep us out. This need to forgive recalls the Parable of the Unforgiving Servant (Matt 18:23-35).

Line 9-10: These requests help in avoiding temptation and evil, which lead us directly away from God's heavenly kingdom.

Lines 11-13: These refer directly to God's awesome power centred in his kingdom.

The one prayer which Jesus taught, the Lord's Prayer, is a prayer about God's heavenly kingdom. All can understand it and pray it. It gives us great encouragement for it reveals to us three of the routes to heaven for which God showers us with tickets. They are through a father's gift to his children; through our desire for God's kingdom; through acts of forgiveness.

First, Jesus informs us that God is our Father. Which earthly father would not long to provide their children with a ticket to heaven? Which is the best gift both in this world and in heaven. God, our heavenly Father, gives us that gift. Jesus provides us with the reassurance that God, as our heavenly Father, is also longing to provide us with that best gift of all. That gift is a ticket to heaven, God's heavenly kingdom. This ticket will be given to us, as a gift, as a consequence of our acknowledging God as our heavenly Father as we do in the Lord's Prayer. Jesus gives no preconditions as to a definition of what our faith in our heavenly Father should be. We just need to declare, through the Lord's Prayer, that God is our heavenly Father. We are only required to acknowledge God as our Father which we do as we say the words "Our Father" in the Lord's Prayer.

Secondly, in praying for the coming of God's kingdom, we acknowledge a desire for his kingdom and a longing to partake of it. This longing reveals our desire for a ticket to heaven. As we have just seen the petitions of the Lord's prayer are concerned with God's heavenly kingdom. They include; "Our Father who art in heaven"; "lead us not into temptation but deliver us from evil" both of which will prevent us accessing God's kingdom; "your kingdom come"; "your will be done on earth as it is in heaven"; "For yours is the kingdom, the power and the glory". In praying for God's will to "be done on earth as it is in heaven," we acknowledge our desire for God's will to be done on earth. This phrase reveals our longing to be in God's heavenly kingdom even now, for where his will is done, there is his kingdom. Thus in this earthly life, we can be in his kingdom by doing his will. For where God's will is being done, there is his kingdom. Such a longing for God's heavenly kingdom will be fulfilled by God, giving us a ticket to heaven.

In Matthew's gospel, Jesus emphasises the need to do the will of God when he teaches; "Not everyone who says to me "Lord, Lord," will enter the kingdom of heaven, but only one who does the will of my Father in heaven" (Mt 7:21).

We ask for the forgiveness of our sins which are a barrier to our entering heaven. In Matthew's gospel, Jesus teaches us that God's mercy and forgiveness remove that barrier and provides us with a ticket to heaven. Jesus also warns us that if we do not also forgive others, God will close our route to heaven. In the next two verses, after the Lord's Prayer, in Matthew's Gospel Jesus says, "For if you forgive others their trespasses, your heavenly Father will also forgive you, but if you do not forgive others, neither will your Father forgive your trespasses" (Mt 6:14,15). Thus, Jesus reminds us of the need to forgive others who "trespass (sin) against us," in other words to forgive those whom we perceive as having wronged ourselves. Jesus teaches us that in forgiving others their sins so also will our sins be forgiven. This need to forgive recalls the Parable of the Unforgiving Servant (Matt 18:23-35). In this parable, Jesus reveals that not forgiving others will bar entrance to God's heavenly kingdom. To refuse to forgive someone demonstrates that, whatever you might say to the contrary, you have no love for them. If you have no love for someone, then heaven, a place full of love, is not the place for you. Hence you bar yourself from heaven. It follows that forgiving others will provide a ticket to heaven. For with sins forgiven by God, then nothing can bar us from heaven. In the Lord's Prayer, we pray for this forgiveness for ourselves. In receiving God's forgiveness, we receive a ticket to heaven.

Through acknowledging God as our heavenly Father and by saying the Lord's Prayer sincerely, God provides us with tickets for three routes into heaven.

Peter states that the purpose and message of Jesus concern eternal life when he says to Jesus, "Lord, to whom can we go? You have the words of eternal life" (Jn 6:68). Paul announces to Timothy that the message of Jesus is one of eternal life and this is the gospel, the Good News which he, Paul, is appointed to proclaim. Paul writes that the Good News of the gospel "has now been revealed through the appearance of our Saviour Christ Jesus, who abolished death and brought life and immortality to light through the gospel. For this gospel, I was appointed a herald and an apostle and a teacher" (2 Tim 1:10,11). Paul is telling Timothy that the message of Jesus, the Good News of Jesus, which Paul calls the gospel, is that Jesus has abolished death. In so doing Jesus has revealed to everyone that immortal life goes on beyond death. Jesus makes it known that eternal life is available to everyone for Jesus has brought "life and immortality to light" (2 Tim1:11). That is the message of Jesus which he, Paul has been appointed a herald, an apostle and a teacher. Jesus reveals the life immortal through his life and teaching, that, says Paul, is the Good News of Jesus.

The message of Jesus is that everyone can have a ticket to heaven. Put in more theological language, the message of Jesus is that God is our heavenly Father who has created everyone for eternal life. Jesus opens God's heavenly kingdom to all. "What happens when we die?" Jesus replies; "You have eternal life." The Good News which Jesus proclaims to every individual is that God has created everyone for eternal life. The challenge to everyone is to live their earthly life with eternal life as its goal.

Some people base their understanding of the message of Jesus on one or a few verses of Scripture. Far better to look at the broad sweep of the whole of the ministry of Jesus to discover the message of Jesus. Doing this we find the following. The whole of the life and ministry of Jesus was bound up in teaching about one thing. Eternal life in God's heavenly kingdom. Jesus announces that this is his message at the start of his ministry. It is the message Jesus proclaims through his parables, his moral teaching, his miracles, and his passion, death and resurrection.

Matthew records that God's kingdom was the centrepiece of the message of Jesus when he states that the good news of the kingdom was at the heart of the message of Jesus. Matthew writes, "Jesus went throughout Galilee, teaching in their synagogues and proclaiming the good news of the kingdom" (Mt 4:23). Matthew unmistakably tells us that Jesus taught about and publicised God's heavenly kingdom throughout Galilee. That was the message of Jesus.

The parables, most of which begin the kingdom of God is like, or the kingdom of heaven is like, unmistakably point to Jesus' message of God's heavenly kingdom and eternal life. Almost 90% of the 46 parables of Jesus teach about God' heavenly kingdom. Hence the well-known summary that the parables are an earthly story with a heavenly meaning. In many parables, Jesus begins explicitly with the words "the kingdom of heaven is like," or" the kingdom of God is like." In starting his parables in this way, using the word is, not will be, Jesus informs us that God's kingdom is a present reality, not something set entirely in the future. From a Christian perspective, the facts of life are that our creation in the womb and our birth are the events which permit us to experience God and his love in this earthly life. Death is the event which enables us to experience God and his love for eternity.

First Aid in Bereavement

Jesus never teaches in his parables; "This is how you must live to have a long and happy life on earth". Jesus never teaches in his parables; "This is how you should live in order to gain peoples respect". Jesus never teaches in his parables; "This is how you should live to become a bishop or church leader." The overwhelming majority of the parables of Jesus teach "the kingdom of heaven is like," or "the kingdom of God is like." The parables are concerned with God's heavenly kingdom, not this life. Jesus uses the things we are familiar with in this life to describe heaven to aid our understanding of heaven. When we read the parables of Jesus, we find almost 90% are about God's heavenly kingdom and eternal life. Hence the well-known saying that the parables are an earthly story with a heavenly meaning. The parables of Jesus teach us about eternal life. Through his parables, Jesus indicates several routes which are available to gain entrance into God's heavenly kingdom.

The Parable of the Good Samaritan, in Luke's gospel (Lk 10:26-37), teaches that the kingdom of heaven is open to all. This parable is probably the best known of the parables of Jesus. In this account, Jesus highlights that the good deeds which we do are one of God's tickets to heaven. Jesus does this when answering the lawyer's question, "What must I do to inherit eternal life?" (Lk 10:25). It is a Good Samaritan who inherits eternal life as a result of a good deed done. The Good Samaritan was a member of another religion, the Samaritan faith. The Jews regarded this at the time of Jesus as the most "diabolical" of other religions. The Jews alive at the time of Jesus regarded Samaritans as having rejected God and as being rejected by God. They were indeed not one of God's chosen people. The Jews regarded Samaritans as belonging to another faith. That such a person from another religion can inherit eternal life shows the endless width of God's mercy. This revelation may shock many Christians today. It would have shocked the Jews who first heard that a despised Samaritan, a member of another religion, could gain entrance to the kingdom of heaven. On the other hand, many Samaritans and other Gentiles on hearing Jesus tell this parable would have rejoiced.

Following on from the Parable of the Good Samaritan, Jesus further emphasises the role which loving our neighbour has in gaining entrance to God's heavenly kingdom in the Parable of the Sheep and the Goats (Matt 25:31-46). In the Parable of the Sheep and the Goats, Jesus makes it plain that entrance into God's heavenly kingdom will be as a result of our deeds. The actions which we take which show help for and kindness to others and so demonstrate our love of our neighbour. Jesus underlines the fundamental significance of these acts of kindness set out in this parable by pointing out that what we do for others, we will find we have done for himself.

The moral teaching of Jesus focuses on living a life that will provide us with tickets to God's heavenly kingdom. His moral teaching is collected together by Matthew in the Sermon on the Mount (Mt 5,6,7). The Beatitudes are the focal point of the sermon and illustrate how the moral teaching of Jesus is focused on God's heavenly kingdom.

In the Beatitudes, Jesus teaches some of the deeds which merit God's blessing. Being blessed by God means we receive all the good things which God can bestow on a person. These good things must include eternal life which is the very best of God's gifts. The Beatitudes are concerned with the whole of life, secular and religious. Amid the hurly-burly of life, Jesus points out the people whose conduct not only is a route into God's heavenly kingdom. Also, it is conduct which places them in God's heavenly kingdom now. Jesus teaches us that these blessings are available now and are not reserved only for some future time. Jesus teaches us, "Blessed are the poor in spirit" (Mt 5:3). Not, "Blessed will be the poor in spirit."

Jesus teaches us; "Blessed are the poor in spirit, for theirs is the kingdom of heaven." (Mt 5:3); "Blessed are those who are persecuted for righteousness' sake, for theirs is the kingdom of heaven" (Matt 5:10). Note that Jesus uses the present tense "are," not will be, meaning that the blessing is received now and on into the future, not just in the future. Jesus uses 'is', present tense, meaning the here and now. The kingdom of heaven is theirs now as well as for the future, following the style of writing of those times. The phrase "for theirs is the kingdom of heaven" is placed after both the first and the penultimate Beatitudes. It indicates that this phrase also applies to all the Beatitudes which lie in between these two as well. This writing custom saved the writer having to repeat this phrase following each of the other Beatitudes. A useful, economic tradition when everything written had to be painstakingly done by hand and writing materials were expensive. The word "is" informs us that the kingdom of heaven is accessible to such people now. The kingdom of heaven can be known now. It is experienced through the joy and fulfilment which arise when doing these things. The conduct described in the Beatitudes is not limited or restricted to Christians. The Beatitudes refer to all who behave in this way, Christian and non-Christian alike. Jesus makes no mention of doing these things in his name, except in the case of the last Beatitude.

"Blessed are the poor in spirit, for theirs is the kingdom of heaven" (Mt 5:3).
"Blessed are those who mourn, for they will be comforted" (Matt 5:4).
"Blessed are the meek, they will inherit the earth" (Matt 5:5).
"Blessed are those who hunger and thirst for righteous-

ness, they will be filled" (Matt 5:6).
"Blessed are the merciful, for they will receive mercy" (Matt 5:7).
"Blessed are the pure in heart, for they will see God" (Matt 5:8).
"Blessed are the peacemakers, for they will be called children of God" (Matt 5:9).
"Blessed are those who are persecuted for righteousness sake, for theirs is the kingdom of heaven" (Matt 5:10).
"Blessed are you when people revile you and persecute you and utter all kinds of evil against you falsely on my account" (Matt 5:11).

To the people of those times, the word blessed meant an inner feeling and awareness of happiness and joy, which was independent of worldly matters. It was a heavenly joy not reliant on earthly events, which leads on to everlasting happiness, satisfaction and contentment. To receive God's blessing means to receive all the good things that God can bestow on a person. To be able to enter God's heavenly kingdom as a citizen is the greatest of the blessings which God can give. The blessings received can be experienced now as well as in the future in God's heavenly kingdom.

In the case of his miracles, Jesus reveals that they, too, are concerned with his message concerning God's heavenly kingdom. Jesus teaches that his miracles disclose the presence of the kingdom of God through the power which he has to perform miracles (Lk 11:14-23). Jesus declares, "if it is by the finger of God that I cast out demons, then the kingdom of God has come to you" (Lk 11:20). The miracles which Jesus performs reveal the power of God and that God's will is being done. Where God's will is being done there is his kingdom. In Matthew's Gospel Jesus also declares that the purpose of his miracles was to proclaim the coming of God's heavenly kingdom. Jesus laments the fact that the people living in the towns where his miracles had been performed, Chorazin, Bethsaida and Capernaum have not repented. The miracles which Jesus did there should have brought forth repentance because the people should have realised that these "mighty works" (Mt11:21) demonstrated the power Jesus had to perform them. This power came not from a natural source but God's heavenly kingdom. This power revealed the kingdom of God had come near, which should have made the witnesses to those miracles realise their need of repentance. By repent, Jesus did not mean to repent of individual sinful acts. Jesus meant to have a complete change of lifestyle to turn away from their present lifestyles and instead embrace a lifestyle based on the values of the kingdom of God (Mt 11:20-24; Lk 10:13-15).

John, in his gospel, describes the miracles of Jesus as signs. Signs that the power of Jesus is not an earthly power but the power of God's heavenly kingdom. John writes, "Now Jesus did many other signs in the presence of his disciples, which are not written in this book. But these are written so that you may come to believe that Jesus is the Messiah, the Son of God and that through believing you may have life in his name" (Jn 20:30,31). The life John mentions here is eternal. John explains that the power revealed by the miracles unveil that Jesus has the clout to make eternal life available to all who believe.

We learn most about the nature and purpose of the life of Jesus through his passion, death and resurrection. Through these events, Jesus proclaims God's everlasting kingdom and its accessibility to all. The passion of Jesus traditionally includes the Last Supper, the agony in the Garden of Gethsemane, the arrest, the trials, the torture and humiliation of Jesus and the crucifixion. At the last supper, Jesus links this meal with God's heavenly kingdom when he declares; "Truly I tell you I will never again drink of the fruit of the vine until that day when I drink it new in the kingdom of God" (Mk 14:25; cf Mt 26:29; Lk 22:18). The suffering of Jesus portrayed in the passion narrative demonstrates that Jesus is fully human. Jesus was reduced to the lowest level of human existence as he hung destitute and seemingly powerless on the cross with his life ebbing away. Jesus experienced what every human being experiences, death. Then on the third day, he rose again. The resurrection of Jesus ratifies that Jesus has power over death. With death overcome, then eternal life is his to bestow on whom he wishes.

The nature of his coming passion and resurrection were known to Jesus. He forewarned his disciples of these coming events, but at the time, they did not comprehend what Jesus was telling them. Mark records three instances where Jesus foretells his coming passion and resurrection to the disciples. For instance, we read, "he was teaching his disciples, saying to them, "The Son of Man is to be betrayed into human hands, and they will kill him, and three days after being killed he will rise again." But they did not understand what he was saying and were afraid to ask him" (Mk 9:31,32; cf Mt 17:22,23, Lk 9:43-45). [See also Mk 8:31,32 cf Mt 16:20-23 and Mk10:32-34, cf Mt 20:17,18, and Lk 18:31-34)]. Jesus knew that his passion was necessary for his resurrection to demonstrate that death was in his control. Thus, his passion, death and resurrection were the concrete proof of the truth of his message. That God has made everyone for eternal life. Through his resurrection, Jesus reveals the power of God to make that message a reality.

Through his passion and resurrection, Jesus reveals that he has the power to defeat death. Peter declares to Jesus "Lord, to whom can we go? You have the words of eternal life" (Jn 6:68). So, like Peter and the disciples, we too come to Jesus because he has the words of eternal life. The message of Jesus to all human beings is that God is the heavenly Father of everyone and God has created everyone for eternal life. This message is the gospel, the Good News, which Jesus came to announce. Jesus came into the world to proclaim how everyone could gain entry to God's kingdom, the kingdom of heaven, to enjoy that eternal life which God makes available to all people.

The whole of the life and ministry of Jesus was bound up in teaching about one thing, eternal life in God's heavenly kingdom. Jesus announces that this is his message at the start of his ministry. It is the message Jesus proclaims through his parables, his moral teaching, his miracles, and his passion death and resurrection.

Let us see how through this message of Good News contained in the gospels, Jesus opens God's heavenly kingdom to all people. Just as boats are made to float on water, so God has made each of us for eternal life. God has not created us to die and be obliterated. We can trust God in this matter for God is the heavenly Father of all people. As we have already discussed in the Lord's Prayer, Jesus teaches us that God is our heavenly Father, the heavenly Father of the whole of humanity. Jesus taught us just the one prayer which anyone in the world can pray at any time. In saying that prayer, a person declares an eternal truth. Each person who says "Our Father who art in heaven" is acknowledging there and then that God is their heavenly Father who has created them for eternal life.

Jesus teaches that eternal life embraces and extends beyond this earthly life. Eternal life is found in God's heavenly kingdom. God's heavenly kingdom is everywhere where God is. Jesus proclaimed this message from the beginning of his ministry. In Mark's gospel, we read, "Now after John was arrested, Jesus came to Galilee, proclaiming the good news of God." The time is fulfilled, and the kingdom of God has come near, repent, and believe in the good news"

(Mark 1:14,15). The kingdom of God is the Good News of God. John, in his gospel, proclaims that Jesus brings eternal life for all who believe. In John's gospel at the beginning of his ministry Jesus speaking to Nicodemus says; "For God so loved the world that he gave his only son, so that everyone who believes in him may not perish but have eternal life" (John 3:16). By declaring that God loves the whole world, that is everyone who is in it, Jesus announces that God's heavenly kingdom is also open to all.

In simplified terms, we speak of living in the kingdom of heaven as "going to heaven". Throughout his ministry, Jesus spoke of the many ways in which people can "go to heaven". That is, enjoy eternal life. In practical terms by his resurrection, Jesus demonstrated that there is eternal life that extends beyond this earthly life.

The message of Jesus is that God created human beings for eternal life. Eternal life or life in heaven is being in the nearer presence of God. It is possible to achieve this in this life as we do those things of which God approves. For where God's will is being done, there is God's kingdom.

Our hearts are troubled at funerals in the face of death because we wonder about what has happened to the deceased whom we knew so well. Funerals also remind us of our mortality and the inevitability of death. Often we also mourn for ourselves; our loss, our fear, and our grief. Jesus allays these fears and worries. Jesus teaches that we have been created for eternal life and that he has prepared a place for us in God's heavenly kingdom, and he will come and take us there. Jesus teaches us, "Do not let your hearts be troubled. Believe in God, believe also in me. In my Father's house, there are many dwelling places. If it were not so, would I have told you that I go to prepare a place for you? And if I go and prepare a place for you, I will come again and will take you to myself, so that where I am, there you may be also" (Jn 14:1-3).

From the beginning of his ministry, Jesus made it clear that he was establishing a heavenly kingdom, not an earthly kingdom. The primary purpose of the ministry of Jesus was to reveal God's heavenly kingdom. Pontius Pilate made the mistake of thinking Jesus wished to establish an earthly kingdom when he had the inscription placed on the cross "The King of the Jews."

Jesus proclaims that God, like every good father, goes out of his way to meet the desires and calm the fears of his children.God meets our greatest desire and calms our deepest fear. The greatest desire of humankind is to live forever. The greatest fear of humanity is death. God, through the teaching of Jesus, reveals to us how to fulfil our greatest desire and live forever. God, reveals to us how to overcome our greatest fear, the fear of death through the resurrection of Jesus as the first fruits of all who die. Jesus overcomes our fears by setting out the many routes which lead to eternal life in God's heavenly kingdom. Jesus does this so that we can know that we are travelling one of those many routes with our ticket to God's place, which is heaven.

Jesus reveals that God has created everyone for eternal life, and we must live our lives with this as our goal. Eternal life is what we should strive for, and God will be only too pleased to see us succeed. The message of Jesus is that everyone can have a ticket to heaven. Jesus tells us in Luke's gospel, "strive for his kingdom………………………for it is your Father's good pleasure to give you the kingdom" (Lk 12:31,32).

For centuries each denomination within the Christian church has each set themselves up to be the gatekeeper for

God's heavenly kingdom. Each setting different carefully prescribed theologically regulated conditions which people, the few, must fulfil. Claiming that such things are necessary before a person can have any hope, in the eyes of that specific denomination of the church, of gaining entrance to God's heavenly kingdom. Thus, the church seeks to strictly limit those who can gain entry to heaven to the few. Whereas Jesus joyfully throws open the gates of heaven to all people, the many, who wish to gain entrance with no such theologically limiting restrictions.

Jesus reveals that there are many ways by which we can gain access to God's presence and a place in his heavenly kingdom. These ways of access as set out by Jesus include the affirmation of Jesus to Nicodemus in John's gospel that being born from above is one of the ways to see the kingdom of God (John 3:3). They include the statement of Jesus in Matthews gospel that Peter has the power to bind and release and holds the keys of the kingdom of heaven (Matt. 16:19). Today these are the two most well-known, and most often quoted, teachings of Jesus, in connection with gaining entrance to God's heavenly kingdom. In addition to these two, there are many other teachings of Jesus, where Jesus explicitly offers a place in God's heavenly kingdom and with it access to God's presence. Jesus teaches us that by taking up our cross and following him, we will find our life, eternal life (Matt. 16:24,25; Mark 8:34,35; Luke 9:23,24). Jesus teaches us that when he returns in Glory, he will repay everyone according to their deeds (Matt. 16:27). To the thief on the cross, Jesus offers him a place in God's kingdom of heaven for his acceptance of and emotional faith in Jesus (Luke 23:43). People who serve the needy will find they have helped Jesus and gain eternal life (Mt25:31-46). The person who loves his neighbour as a 'Good Samaritan' will gain access to God's heavenly kingdom (Lk10:25-37). Jesus sets out the conduct which will receive God's blessing in his teaching in the Beatitudes (Mt5:1-12). To receive God's Blessing is to receive all the good things which God wishes to bestow. These good things will and must include a place in God's heavenly kingdom, for this is the greatest blessing which God can give. Most of the parables of Jesus teach about the kingdom of God and eternal life, revealing yet more routes into God's heavenly kingdom.

Other sections of the New Testament expand and underscore this teaching of Jesus. Paul in his Epistles writes about routes into the kingdom of heaven, including justification by faith (Gal. 3:24), love (1 Cor 13), through the Holy Spirit (Gal. 6:8) and good deeds (Rom 2:6,7). In the Book of Revelation at the Final Judgement, the writer tells us that our deeds will determine whether or not we have the companionship of God in the new earth and new heaven which God will create (Rev 20:12). The first letter of John teaches that if we love one another God abides in us(1 John 4:16) and if we do the will of God (1 John 2:17), then we will be welcomed into the kingdom of heaven.

Jesus proclaimed that the many routes into the kingdom of heaven were available to and being used by all, not just the few. Witness the words of Jesus to the religious leaders of his time, the chief priests and elders. They sought to restrict people's access to God and therefore, entry into God's heavenly kingdom, to the few, by their religious rules and customs. Jesus says to them, "Truly I tell you the tax-collectors and the prostitutes are going into the kingdom of God ahead of you" (Matt 21:31). These are not people whom those leaders of religious opinions and religious traditions would expect to find in God's heavenly kingdom. Jesus is telling us that we will find people in heaven whom religious leaders would not expect to find there. Nor would religious traditions define them as followers of Jesus and one of God's chosen people.

We should give equal weight to all that Jesus taught about gaining entrance into heaven. In this way, we avoid allowing selected passages of scripture to become too prominent and colour our interpretation of all that Jesus taught. Similarly, we should not allow the whole spectrum of what Jesus taught to be pruned to fit into the traditions of one of the many church denominations. Instead, we should accept all that Jesus taught as having equal weight and influence. Much of what Jesus taught was in self-contained units, each sufficient for its first audience. We should give equal weight to each standalone section of the teaching of Jesus and also see it as being sufficient on its own merits for ourselves and others. When we do this, we discover that Jesus describes many routes which lead to God's kingdom of heaven. We also find that Jesus spent most of his ministry not teaching about this earthly life but teaching about eternal life and the kingdom of heaven. On the occasions on which Jesus spoke about this human life, it was usually in connection with or to explain eternal life.

At times Jesus speaks of the need for belief in himself, without giving a clear definition of that belief. Unlike the definitions found in the later creeds of the church. In St John's gospel, Jesus tells us "I am the resurrection and the life. Those who believe in me, even though they die will live, and everyone who lives and believes in me will never die" (John 11:25). On another occasion, Jesus declares, "God so loved the world that he gave his only Son, so that everyone who believes in him may not perish but may have eternal life" (John 3:16). In these two verses, Jesus reveals that all can gain eternal life through a belief in himself.

Nevertheless, many people could not express in words their faith in Jesus because they have never heard of him. They are unaware of Jesus for many reasons, including the geography of where they live and the time in history when they lived.

In the next chapter, we shall see that God has provided for them because faith in Jesus can and does encompass all people. Faith in Jesus can be as equally well expressed in deeds as it has been traditionally expressed in words. These good deeds reveal conformity to the teaching of Jesus to love our neighbour.

Faith in what Jesus proclaimed finds expression through doing the good deeds which Jesus advocated as well as expression through the traditional verbal expressions of faith. Thus, from the time when human beings first evolved to walk on this earth. It was possible to receive a ticket to heaven by loving your neighbour. Through loving your neighbour, a person demonstrates that they have the mind of Christ. It represents faith in what Jesus stood for, for they are doing what Jesus revealed to be the way God wants people to live.

Some of the deeds which we do, which will gain eternal life are set out by Jesus in the Beatitudes (Matt 5:1-11). There Jesus describes some of the many routes which people are following which lead to heaven. In the Beatitudes, Jesus sets out certain deeds. God will bless the people who carry out these actions. God's blessing is the bestowing on a person of all the good things which God can bestow. This blessing must include God's gift of life in his kingdom. The very best of God's good gifts. **Jesus tells us in Luke's gospel, "for it is your Father's good pleasure to give you the kingdom" (Lk 12:32).** In his kingdom, we have eternal life the greatest of the good things which God can bestow

Jesus not only taught about life beyond death, but he rose from the dead. The resurrection of Jesus was proof of what he taught. It is one thing to talk about something. It is another thing to do it. Golfers will talk about how far they can drive a golf ball. When they stand on the tee and hit the golf ball, the truth is revealed. Jesus not only talks about and teaches us about eternal life, but on the first Easter Day, Jesus rose from the dead. The answer which Jesus gives us to the question, "What happens when we die?" is, "You have eternal life." Jesus did not just talk about eternal life. Jesus rose from the dead, demonstrating that eternal life is a reality. The message of Jesus is that God, our heavenly father, has created everyone for eternal life and showered everyone with tickets for the many ways which lead to heaven. We must see our mourning within this perspective. It is a perspective which allows us to see that God can wipe away every tear for Jesus teaches us that God's plan is to provide everyone with a ticket to heaven. Belief in this enables a mourner to see that their loved one has embraced that eternal life which God wishes everyone to enjoy. It is also the pathway which the mourner is already on to join their lost loved one. God does indeed wipe away every tear for "Death will be no more; mourning and crying and pain will be no more" (Rev 21:4). For to the question "What happens when we die?" Jesus' answer is, "You have eternal life." Where there is no more mourning or crying or pain.

# 20 THE CHRISTIAN FAITH AND ETERNAL LIFE

Jesus proclaims that anyone who puts their faith in him will gain eternal life. In the gospels, Jesus does not give us an all-embracing definition of what that faith is but endorses three aspects of faith which are all routes to heaven. The first is the faith of the intellect as expressed, for example, by Peter at Caesarea Philippi (Mt 16:15,16). The church extended this faith to include philosophical and theological statements, for example, in the form of a creed or dogmas. The second, is the faith of the emotions, as demonstrated by the Sinful Woman at the Pharisee's house (Lk 7:36-50). This faith can also be expressed as a verbal statement declaring a personal relationship with Jesus, for example, when a person acknowledges that Jesus is their saviour. The third aspect is the faith of actions expressed through practical acts showing the love of neighbour as taught by Jesus as in the Parable of the Sheep and the Goats (Mt 25:31-46). Such deeds, whether done in the name of Jesus or not demonstrate faith in or solidarity with Jesus through deeds done. In just the same way as the other two express faith in or solidarity with Jesus through spoken or written words.

This third way, the faith of actions, opens God's salvation to all. The faith of actions enables all people, Christian and non-Christian, to reveal their solidarity with Jesus and their acceptance of his values. This faith is revealed through their love of their neighbours shown through doing good deeds. It is a part of God's plan for the salvation of all people, as taught in the Parable of the Good Samaritan (Lk 10:25-37).

John N Greenwood

**The faith of actions brings Christians together, who otherwise are kept separated by statements defining the faith of the intellect or the faith of the emotions of each specific Christian denomination.**

People respond to Jesus by putting their faith in him. In the gospels, Jesus tells us that through faith in him, we will gain eternal life. Jesus says, "For God so loved the world that he gave his only Son, so that everyone who believes in him may not perish but may have eternal life" (Jn 3:16). Jesus does not define this faith in the form of dogma or creed. What Jesus does do is to set out the many routes by which we can travel to God's heavenly kingdom and there enjoy that eternal life. These were described in the last chapter. In describing these routes, Jesus endorses three expressions of faith. The faith of the intellect, for example, Peter's confession at Caesarea Phillipi (Mt 16:15,16). The faith of the emotions as demonstrated by the Sinful Woman in the Pharisee's house (Lk 7:36-50). The faith of actions as taught by Jesus in the Parable of the Sheep and the Goats (Mt 25:31-46). By looking at the routes, Jesus sets down, which lead to God's heavenly kingdom; we can see that Jesus validates these three ways of expressing faith in him. Each expression can stand alone or be interwoven with the others.

Historically the church has formulated oral confessions of faith. In the 21st century, most Christians would see an oral statement expressing their faith as falling into one of two categories. Either a declaration of the faith of the intellect, for example, a creed or specific church dogmas. Or, as a statement of the faith of the emotions based on a personal relationship with Jesus, for example, a statement such as, "Jesus is my saviour," or "Jesus is my brother and friend." Such a personal relationship has usually come about as a result of being "born again" or some similar conversion experience. The faith of the emotions is felt from the heart, but the faith of the intellect is understood and reasoned by the mind.

Jesus also validates the third expression of faith, the faith of actions. Jesus did not leave any concise verbal declaration of faith and command his followers to "repeat after me". Jesus was not concerned with setting down a verbal definition of what faith in himself involved which people could then write down or memorise. Jesus commands his followers to "follow after me", not "repeat after me". It leads to the third way of expressing faith in Jesus, the faith of actions. It is demonstrated by following Jesus by putting into practice what he taught and by following his example. This expression of faith traditionally has no authorised verbal expression, for instance, in a creed or dogma. Later it will be seen how good deeds, the visible sign of the faith of actions, demonstrate faith in and solidarity with Jesus in a very similar way to a verbal statement of faith. These good deeds show love for our neighbour as taught by Jesus. They may be done in the name of Jesus or not as the case may be.

Peter declares to Jesus "Lord, to whom can we go? You have the words of eternal life" (Jn 6:68). So, like the disciples, we too come to Jesus because he has the words of eternal life. Coming to Jesus, for this reason, is in itself an expression of our emotional faith in Jesus. Jesus does have the words to eternal life. In the gospels, Jesus teaches us that God showers us with tickets to travel the many routes God provides, which lead to eternal life in his heavenly kingdom. This teaching of Jesus is his words of eternal life. In St John's gospel, Jesus tells us "I am the resurrection and the life. Those who believe in me, even though they die will live, and everyone who lives and believes in me will never die" (John 10:25). On another occasion, Jesus declares, "God so loved the world that he gave his only Son, so that everyone who believes in him may not perish but may have eternal life" (John 3:16). Through these two verses, Jesus teaches us that all who wish to can gain eternal life through faith in him. Following these two statements, Jesus does not go on to give a precise definition to explain the nature of the faith or define the belief to which he refers. Over time this belief in Jesus has traditionally come to be accepted as being expressed in the verbal form of either the faith of the intellect or the faith of the emotions. These two verbal expressions of faith, the faith of the intellect and the faith of the emotions are not mutually exclusive, and there is overlap in peoples experience and utilisation of them. We will examine below how belief in Jesus can also be expressed in that third way through the good deeds of the faith of actions.

The historical changes in intellectual faith have occurred because nowhere in the gospels does Jesus set out a verbal definition or description of faith in a similar form to that found in one of the creeds in use today. Jesus does not define the Christian faith for Christians. Instead in the gospels, we read of a person's faith being expressed in a variety of circumstances and contexts, but Jesus gives no overarching summary linking together all the separate and different aspects of the Christian faith.

Described below are modern working definitions of these three expressions of faith which Jesus validates. Each one enables that belief in Jesus, which ensures that a person will not die but have eternal life. Where appropriate, the extent of the additions by the church to their original gospel meanings are given, which are significant in the case of the faith of the intellect.

**The faith of the intellect**

Today the faith of the intellect is an academic faith on which an exam could be set with right or wrong answers. It

First Aid in Bereavement

is based on statements set down in the Bible and the creeds, and the dogmas and doctrines of a specific church. It is the primary focus of belief in the Roman Catholic and Eastern Orthodox branches of Christianity. The Eastern Orthodox Church is a family of thirteen churches each based on a country, e.g. Russian Orthodox Church, Greek Orthodox Church, Romanian Orthodox Church. Each runs its affairs, but as a group, they have a standard set of beliefs. Each has its patriarch, with the Patriarch of Constantinople being seen as the first amongst equals.

The Catechism of the Roman Catholic Church published in 1992 contains almost 3000 points of dogma and doctrine. Each specific national Eastern Orthodox Church adheres to one of the Catechisms of that national branch of the church which contain many hundreds of points of dogma and doctrine. The Catechism of Saint Philaret of Moscow of 1839 has just over 600 points of dogma and doctrine. These Catechisms confirm how the faith of the intellect has grown significantly in content since New Testament times. These additional dogmas and doctrines were drawn up by the many church councils which met over the centuries to define the official teaching of the church. There underlying purpose was to ward off heresy. All dogmas are included in doctrine, but not all doctrine is set out as dogma. The doctrines of a specific church encompass the whole of the teaching of that church on many different topics. The dogmas of a particular church are the more authoritative teaching of a church which must not be questioned. They are essential to the faith of that church and failure to follow them can result in excommunication from that church.

The Nicene Creed, drawn up in 325, is the most widely accepted concise expression of the faith of the intellect amongst the three branches of the Christian church. The Nicene Creed, also known as the Nicene-

Constantinopolitan Creed, is the only ecumenical creed accepted by the Eastern Orthodox, Roman Catholic, Anglican and major Protestant churches. In addition to the Nicene Creed, the three main branches of the Christian Church set down their dogmas, doctrines and traditions which they hold as having a place in their intellectual faith. In the case of the Protestant churches, traditional expressions of the faith of the intellect include their specific declarations of faith. For instance, in addition to the creeds, the Church of England set down the 39 Articles of Religion at a Church Convocation in 1563 under Matthew Parker, Archbishop of Canterbury. An Act of Parliament finalised them in 1571. Some examples of the many denominational statements of faith set down include Zwingli's Sixty-Seven Articles (1523) being one of the first; the Augsburg Confession (1530) of the Lutheran Church presented by German Lutheran princes to Emperor Charles $5^{th}$ at Diet of Augsberg in their dispute with the Medieval Roman Catholic Church; the Geneva Confession of Faith (1536) by John Calvin for his church in Geneva. These statements are described as being subordinate to scripture.

In the case of the Roman Catholic Church, these additional traditional expressions of faith include the pronouncements of ancient church councils such as the Council of Nicaea (325); the declarations of only the historic Roman Catholic church councils most importantly the Council of Trent (1545-1563); and some papal dogmas. These declarations are perceived as explaining and enhancing scripture, rather than being subordinate to Scripture.

In the case of the Eastern Orthodox Church, these traditional expressions of faith also include the verdicts of ancient church councils, for example, the Council of Nicaea (325) and only the historic councils of the Eastern Orthodox Church such as the Synod of Constantinople (1484). These pronouncements are also perceived as explaining and enhancing scripture, rather than being subordinate to it.

These pronouncements arising from different councils and church bodies give rise to differences in the faith of the intellect between the three branches of the church.

The different interpretations of the Bible have also lead to differences in the faith of the intellect of the three branches. All three branches of the church accept the authority of the Bible, in teaching the truth about God. Still, differences in its interpretation give rise to different doctrines. The Roman Catholic and Eastern Orthodox Church interpret scripture in the light of the teaching of their historical church traditions, which they see as being guided by God. For Protestant Christians, sola scriptura (scripture alone) is a foundational dogma. It means that scripture is the only infallible truth about the Christian religion and, rather than historical church councils and traditions being allowed to interpret scripture. Then scripture must reform ancient church councils and traditions to bring them back in line with scripture. Thus, the decisions of church councils and church dignitaries are trumped by scripture rather than the other way around when differences occur between scripture and church teaching. Protestantism understands the infallibility of scripture as being ensured by the search for and the acceptance of the best discernible texts and the witness of the Holy Spirit in the heart of the individual Christian.

A gospel example of the faith of the intellect acknowledged by Jesus is Peter's confession at Caesarea Philippi (Mt 16:13-20; Mk 8:27-30; Lk 9:18-20). Peter declares to Jesus, "You are the Messiah, the Son of the living God" (Mt 16:16). Also, Jesus makes various statements about himself at different points in his ministry. Declarations which require intellectual belief by Christians, his followers. For instance, Jesus states that he is the Son of God. In John's gospel, we read, "Jesus said to them, "Very truly, I tell you, the Son can do nothing on his own, but only what he sees the Father doing: for whatever the Father does the Son does likewise" (Jn 5:19). In John's gospel, Jesus says, "Believe in God, believe also in me" (Jn 14:1). Thus, faith or belief in Jesus requires our having complete trust, confidence and spiritual conviction in Jesus just as we have in God. Jesus describes God and himself as being one. Jesus says, "The Father and I are one" (John 10:30). Thus, our intellectual faith must accept that Jesus and God are one. Intellectual faith also includes the belief in the whole of the life and teaching of Jesus, including his death and resurrection.

**The faith of the emotions**

The rediscovery of the faith of the emotions occurred at the Reformation. Its roots can be traced back to the New Testament. It is found in the Pharisee's house when a sinful woman washes the feet of Jesus with her tears and wipes them with her hair. Jesus says to her; "Your faith has saved you. Go in peace" (Luke 7:50). Her tears show that it is a faith of the emotions based on her fellowship with Jesus. It is an emotional faith which Jesus speaks about to Nicodemus when he says to him, "You must be born from above" (Jn 3:7). It is an emotional faith which Paul taught, for example, in his letter to the Galatians. In the opening verses of his letter, Paul expresses his surprise that the Galatians are turning from the gospel which he taught (Gal 1:6-10). Paul reminds them that the gospel he taught was "justification by faith." That is the inward emotional awareness that the merits of the death of Christ on the cross have paid the price of our sins and restored us to be righteous in God's eyes and at peace with God. Paul writes, "we know that a person is justified not by the works of the law but through faith in Jesus Christ" (Gal 2:16).

Paul is the author of the church's theology of "justification by faith". It is a significant theme in his Epistles to the Romans and the Galatians and is mentioned in other Epistles. A person knows in their heart that they are "justified by faith". Being "justified by faith" results from a person's inner feeling that they are saved. It is the faith of the emotions. The expression of the faith of the emotions disappeared with the fall from prominence of the theology of "justification by faith" in the writings and mission of the early church. Paul wrote in his letter to the Romans about his theology of "justification by faith". Yet despite Paul's presence for a time in Rome and Paul's teaching being known in Rome, one of the major centres of Christianity in the early church, it became forgotten. It is not mentioned in the Nicene Creed or other early Biblical, creedal statements. It is not a significant theme in the mission and life of the early church. It was not recovered until the Reformation.

In the gospels, Jesus spoke of belief or faith without clearly defining it in the form of a creed. The best example of belief, which Jesus himself acknowledges as such, is that of the centurion whose servant Jesus heals (Luke 7:1-10; Mt 8:5-13). Jesus declares; "I tell you, not even in Israel have I found such faith" (Luke 7:9). With such faith, the centurion certainly had a ticket to heaven. Neither Jesus nor the centurion give a creed like definition of that faith or explain the origin or nature of that faith. We are left to determine the nature of that faith for ourselves. This incident involves a faith which is similar to that of the thief crucified with Jesus. It is a faith felt from inside, from the heart. The faith that Jesus has the love and the power to do all that is necessary, for the circumstances, to ensure a successful outcome. It is an example of the faith of the emotions.

The faith of the emotions was revived with the rediscovery by Martin Luther (1483-1546) of Paul's teaching on "justification by faith". The re-emergence of the faith of the emotions brought a new dimension to the doctrines of worldwide Christianity.

The faith of the emotions is felt most powerfully through our inner feelings on being born again or being converted. This faith stems from the heart and is experienced through our emotions. It empowers a person to trust, as the truth, their inner thoughts and feelings about their salvation. It continues as a faith, which is based on fellowship and friendship with Jesus. This faith arises in response to his saving death on the cross to secure our salvation. The faith of the emotions can be set down as a verbal statement of personal faith in Jesus based on a person's own experience of Jesus in their present lifetime. It usually follows on from a conversion experience, such as being "born again." This faith has traditionally verbally been expressed through words such as "I know that Jesus is my saviour," or "I have been born again," or "I know that Jesus is alive today," or "My faith in Jesus has saved me." The faith of the emotions is grounded on the affirmation by Martin Luther that we are "justified by faith" and faith alone.It enables a person, through their feelings, to know the personality and presence of Jesus as a friend or brother would be recognised and acknowledged.

It finds the most significant expression in the Protestant branch of the church. It found advancement through Evangelicalism. Today Evangelicalism is a worldwide movement within Protestantism which transcends denominational barriers. It grew out of the First Great Awakening or Evangelical Revival, a series of Protestant Christian revivals which occurred in Britain and its thirteen North American colonies in the 1730s and 1740s. The early founders were John Wesley (1703-1791), his brother

Charles Wesley (1707-1788) and George Whitfield (1714-1770), all were Anglican clergymen who went on to be the founders of Methodism, and Jonathan Edwards (1703-1758) an American Congregationalist and revivalist preacher. The early movement had close links with the Moravian Church and the Lutheran pietist movement. The foundation of Evangelicalism is Luther's declaration that we are "justified by faith" and faith alone (sola fide -by faith alone). Central to it is the "born again" or conversion experience seen as being necessary for salvation. It is attendant on the belief that a person's salvation is attained, through the grace of God (sola gratia – by grace alone) and through faith in the death of Jesus to pay the price for their sins (sola fide - faith alone). This belief is brought about by the grace of God acting in a person's heart. Thus the person can claim no merit for themselves because God is the author of their faith. Well known modern leaders of this Evangelicalism include Billy Graham. Gospel examples of the faith of the emotions acknowledged by Jesus include the Sinful Woman in the Pharisee's house (Lk 7:36-50); The Centurion whose Servant was Healed (Mk 8:2-13; Lk 7:1-10); the Crucified Thief (Lk 23:39-43). The declaration by Jesus to Nicodemus that he must be "born from above" (Jn 3:3) is also an example of the faith of the emotions.

**The faith of actions**

The faith of actions is a practical faith expressed in deeds done rather than words spoken. It manifests itself through the realisation of what needs to be done in any situation to show the love of a neighbour and then to do it. It might be as common as holding a door open for someone or as rare as risking one's own life to secure someone's safety. It is found being expressed through all manner of charitable and caring actions.

As a result of acknowledging that such good deeds done can also be seen as expressing faith in Jesus. Then we realise that God, because of his love for the world and everyone in it, provides this route of faith to his heavenly kingdom, which is open to everyone. Everyone includes Christians and non-Christians alike. Jesus teaches this in the gospel accounts, witness the Parable of the Good Samaritan (Lk 10:25-37). The Good Samaritan undoubtedly was the sort o person who had a ticket to God's heavenly kingdom. The Good Samaritan was a member of another religion, the Samaritan faith. The Jews in Biblical times despised and hated the Samaritans because of their rejection of the Jewish faith.

Following on from the Parable of the Good Samaritan, Jesus further emphasises the role which loving our neighbour has in gaining entrance to God's heavenly kingdom in the Parable of the Sheep and the Goats (Matt 25:31-46). In the Parable of the Sheep and the Goats, Jesus makes it plain that entrance into God's heavenly kingdom will be as a result of our deeds. The actions which we take which show help for and kindness to others and so demonstrate our love of our neighbour. Jesus underlines the full significance of these acts of kindness set out in this parable by pointing out that what we do for others, we will find we have done for himself. In this parable, Jesus lists six ways in which we can help others; in other words, love our neighbour. These six ways cover what is needed to sustain a full and happy life. They are food, drink, clothing, medical aid, together with meeting a person's emotional needs of befriending by welcoming the stranger and visiting the prisoner. Jesus informs us, "for I was hungry and you gave me food, I was thirsty and you gave me something to drink, I was a stranger, and you welcomed me, I was naked, and you gave me clothing, I was sick, and you took care of me, I was in prison and you visited me."(Matt. 25:35,36). These six examples do not limit our love to these six tasks.

Rather they show that our love should be boundless and have no limits. Our love should extend to providing help with all that is needed to live a full and satisfying life. In fact, on another occasion Jesus teaches us that our love must even include the love of our enemies; "But I say to you, love your enemies and pray for those who persecute you," (Matt. 5:44). This teaching transcends every religion. It applies to all, Christians and non-Christians alike, just as it applied to Jew and non-Jew (gentile) alike who were the first people to hear the teaching of Jesus. Jesus does not require those who minister to the needy to do it in his name. He just requires that people do it. This parable applies to all people, Christians and non-Christians. People of other faiths will gain entrance to heaven by helping others in these ways. Jesus saves his harshest words for the righteous, those who thought they were God's chosen people, who failed to help those in need. Jesus condemns the Pharisees for keeping the minutia of the law but neglecting justice and mercy (Mt 23:23). Jesus told the parable of the Pharisee and the Tax Collector against those who were self-righteous and regarded others with contempt (Lk 18:9-14).

The third expression of faith, the faith of actions, is based on doing good deeds here and now. This faith over the centuries of church history has been less well emphasised. It has not, for example, found expression in the creeds of the church. Nor has it been given a similar formal verbal declaration of faith as the first two have. Though this faith can be verbally expressed, for example, "I believe in Jesus because he leads me to do the good deeds which I do." This third expression of faith has a vital part to play in affirming the validity of the other two expressions of faith. No matter how eloquently a person expresses their faith. If they do not display the faith of actions in their day to day living, their verbal expression of faith will be seen as being a fraud. This third expression of faith is revealed through good deeds, such as the ones described in the Beatitudes, which all spring from our Lord's command to love our neighbour. This expression of faith, as we have seen, encompasses non-Christians as well as Christians.

Jesus teaches us just one prayer, the Lord's Prayer. That one prayer acknowledges that God is the Father of all people. God is the heavenly Father of all people. As any father would, God wants all his children to come around to his place. God wants all his children to enter his heavenly kingdom. It should come as no surprise, therefore that God provides the route of the faith of actions as a means of entry into his heavenly kingdom. For such a faith encompasses all people, Christian and non-Christian alike. That God is our heavenly Father gives us the sure knowledge that God will protect and care for everyone in his family of humankind. Just as the perfect earthly father would care for his family, we know that God our heavenly Father who has created us for eternal life will do all that he can to ensure that all people can enjoy living in his heavenly home, both now and for eternity, just as any father would. The provision of the route through the faith of actions is a testimony of the love of our heavenly Father for all people, for God is love (1 John 4:8). Through the faith of actions, everyone, Christian and non-Christian alike can gain entrance into God's heavenly kingdom.

Jesus lived at a specific time in history and a particular country. Many people are in no position to declare a verbal confession of faith in Jesus. As a result of the historical time in which they lived and/or as a result of the beliefs of the society or the geographical location into which they were born. It raises the question of the salvation of all those people who could not know of the teaching of Jesus through such "accidents" of history and geography. Regarding accidents of history and geography, after his life, death and resurrection, it was many centuries before Jesus was made known to people throughout the world. Also, many people today find that the church, as a human institution, does not meet their spiritual needs. It might be because of its "bloody" history of wars, Crusades and the burning at the stake of so-called heretics. Or recent child abuse scandals and cover-ups or other reasons. All of this raises some questions.

If God, whom Jesus teaches us, is a God of love and the heavenly Father of all people. Then is God going to leave some people totally out of his plans for salvation? Are so many people going to be frozen out of salvation because of an accident of history and/or geography or the failure of the church? The answer to that question can only be an emphatic no.

These people are all able to express their faith through the faith of actions. This third way of faith through actions opens God's salvation to all. The faith of actions enables all people to reveal their solidarity with Jesus, and their belief in his values through the love of their neighbours revealed through doing good deeds. It is part of God's plan for the salvation of all.

In the Parable of the Good Samaritan if Jesus had wished to emphasise that eternal life was only available to a few people, those who were traditionally regarded as God's people. Then Jesus could just as easily have chosen a fellow Jew as the hero. He could have selected perhaps a tax collector or someone from another section of Jewish society who were regarded as being outcasts for the role of the Good Samaritan. Alternatively, maybe one of his followers, who could then be seen as setting a Christian example. Jesus chose a member of another religion, the Samaritan faith, to be the Good Samaritan. It indisputably reveals that God's heavenly kingdom is open to all, Christian and non-Christian alike. This third way of expressing faith in Jesus, the faith of actions, provides a route to salvation for all people.

The faith of actions is inextricably linked to the two verbal expressions of faith. It is universally accepted that unless a person backs up their verbal expression of their faith of the intellect or faith of the emotions, with the faith of actions through doing good deeds. Then those two verbal expressions of faith will be perceived as being empty and futile declarations of faith. The faith of actions expressed through good deeds is needed to validate a person's verbal statement of their faith. Good deeds, therefore, have an indispensable part to play in a person's faith; however, that faith is expressed.

The good deeds done, as advocated by Jesus, demonstrate that a person is living by the values of Jesus. Living by the values of Jesus expresses solidarity with Jesus through performing the good deeds which he taught. It is akin to how a verbal statement of faith also shows solidarity with what Jesus taught. Thus, living by the values of Jesus revealed by our deeds is a third way of expressing faith or belief in Jesus. Living by the values which Jesus proclaims, demonstrates faith in those values and therefore faith in Jesus who advocates those values. These values which Jesus sets out in his teaching are governed by his command to love our neighbours.

The good deeds done in the name of Jesus or the same good deeds done by someone who does not know Jesus both reveal faith in the values of God, which Jesus proclaims and stands for. Doing such good deeds shows a total acceptance, we can also say a belief, in what Jesus stands for and what he came to proclaim. That is that we should love our neighbour as ourselves. On this basis, good deeds are a third way of expressing faith in Jesus and God. They are valid and concrete proof that God's will is being done, whether the good deeds are done in the name of God or not. They reveal and spread the love and goodness which God wants to abound in his world. It can also be argued that since good deeds are required to validate a person's verbal statement of faith. Then the faith of actions is at least equal to if not more trustworthy and genuine than the other two expressions of faith. For no matter how stridently or eloquently someone declares their faith verbally, other people will judge its validity on the good deeds which they do.

God, through his love for everyone, fills the void of how people can gain entrance into his heavenly kingdom through faith when they have never heard of or never had the chance to learn about himself or Jesus. He does this as a result of faith being able to be expressed through doing good deeds. Good deeds done by anyone, Christian or non-Christian, reveals to the world how God wants people to live with one another. It sets before others an example of how they ought to live — thus encouraging people to live as God intends people to live, in love and fellowship with one another. Jesus emphasises the role of good deeds when he declares, "let your light shine before others, so that they may see your good works and give glory to your Father in heaven" (Mt 5:16). Jesus teaches us that it is the works or deeds of Christians, not their statements of faith which unequivocally shine forth God's light to the world. Such right actions or good deeds are the practical expressions of what Jesus proclaimed to be how we should live to reveal God and his goodness to the world. In doing this, people fulfil the will of God. Where God's will is being done, there is his kingdom.

Further, the love which such good deeds reveal also reveals God for God is love (1 Jn 4:16). However well expressed, an assemblage of intellectual beliefs or emotional feelings does not define God. Love defines God. Thus, our faith in

Jesus and God can be expressed through the love shown in good deeds just as, it can be expressed in words. In this way, God, our heavenly Father, enables everyone, through their good deeds, to receive a ticket to heaven. For their good deeds reveal they are living here and now by the values of God which will last forever. Thus, from the time when human beings first evolved to walk on this planet, it was possible to receive a ticket to heaven by loving your neighbour. Through loving their neighbour, a person demonstrates that they have the mind of Christ. They are living by what Jesus revealed to be the values of God and the way God wants people to live. By living the way, God wants a person to live guarantees them their ticket to heaven.

The roles played by good deeds and verbal statements of faith was also an issue in New Testament times. James, in his Epistle, stresses the need for works or, as we would say today, good deeds. James points out the need for Christians to be doers of good deeds, not just passive hearers of the good news (James 1:19-27). James also declares that faith without good deeds is dead. James writes, "So faith by itself if it has no works, is dead" (James 2:17). Good deeds are the practical expression of the love which we have for our neighbour. Paul, the author of the doctrine of "justification by faith," stresses that there is a role of good deeds. Paul did not go as far as Luther in stating that justification was by faith alone (sola fide). Paul acknowledged the role of good deeds. Paul writes "For he (God) will repay according to each one's deeds: to those who by patiently doing good seek for glory and honour and immortality, he will give eternal life" (Rom 2:6,7).

Christians may place undue emphasis on one of the two verbal statements of faith, the faith of the intellect or the faith of the emotions. It arises because a Christian having experienced God in one of these ways, concludes that everyone else can also only experience God in that one way. Whereas experiencing God is open to everyone in many ways. Jesus warns us against coming to the view that entry into God's heavenly kingdom will be limited to the few who also think as we do. Jesus reveals the diversity of the people entering the kingdom of heaven when he says to the chief priests and elders who question him; "The tax collectors and prostitutes are getting into the kingdom of God ahead of you" (Matt. 21:31). Jesus does not indicate that these people have now become Christians.

There is only one God, but we encounter him in many ways. The value of the Doctrine of the Trinity to Christians is that it reminds us that we will encounter God in different ways. We encounter God, the creator as science reveals the working of his creation, and we marvel at the beauty and structure of the natural world and the universe. We encounter God as we come to appreciate him as our heavenly Father as we seek to do our heavenly Father's will. We encounter God as we realise that Jesus gave his life for us and as a result of his resurrection, he is our constant travelling companion in this life as we strive to do the things Jesus taught and did. We encounter God as we experience the power of the Holy Spirit, changing us and empowering us to serve God. We encounter God in the acts of love which we see in others and as we love and care for our neighbour.

Down the centuries the church has looked to emphasise that the things of God are only done in churches and chapels and similar buildings. In such places, matters relating to the faith of the intellect and the faith of the emotions have centre stage. The faith of actions, however, is to be found everywhere. Through the faith of actions, the things of God are being done everywhere.

People express their love of their neighbour through their work; for instance, people working in the caring professions such as are to be found in the NHS. This work may not be being done in the name of Jesus or God, but it is the faith of actions in action. Whatever a person's work is, it is possible to show the love of neighbour through the way other people are treated during a days work. People express the love of neighbour through charity work. People show the love of neighbour through neighbourliness in their community. The love which binds families together is a further example of the faith of actions. Where the love of others is being shown, there is the faith of actions. Even though in many cases, these actions will not be being done in the name of Jesus or God.

Of the three aspects of faith, it is only the faith of actions which draws Christians together. It enables them to work as one, as Christians fulfil the command of Jesus to love your neighbour. This faith empowers Christians to work together in many situations. The faith of actions brings Christians together in community projects and charitable organisations as diverse as food banks and the Samaritans. It fulfils the prayer of Jesus, "I ask.............that they all may be one. As you, Father, are in me, and I am in you" (Jn 17:20,21). Jesus wanted his followers to be one united body. Christians being one body is a significant theme in the Epistles of Paul (1 Cor 10:17, Eph 2:16, Col 3:15, Gal 3:28). In his Epistle to the Romans, Paul writes, "so we, who are many, are one body in Christ, and individually we are members one of another" (Rom 12:5).

Further, the faith of actions not only enables Christians to work together. It also allows non-Christians, who through showing their love of their neighbour, show they have the values of Christ, to work with Christians who also have the values of Christ. It is occurring in many communities and charitable organisations.

Many Christians are concerned about how to talk to others about their faith. The faith of actions neatly overcomes this dilemma. For in demonstrating the faith of actions, Christians reveal their love for others which is the bedrock of the Christian faith. In whatever situation a Christian finds themselves in, then their faith of actions has a part to play. For through it, a Christian reveals their faith, through the good deeds which they do and the care and compassion which they show for work colleagues and how they treat other people with love. Jesus says, "let your light shine before others, so that they may see your good works and give glory to your Father in heaven" (Mt 5:16).

The two verbal expressions of faith have evolved in such a way as to disunite and divide rather than unite Christians. In the case of the faith of the intellect, the religious truth which informs that intellectual belief is determined in different ways by the three major branches of Christianity. Thus, ensuring that there will be differences in the intellectual faith of each branch. It supports and ensures disunity between the three branches. The faith of the emotions though predominant in Evangelical Protestantism is questioned and shunned by the other two branches of the church, as it is not a part of their ancient traditions.

A study of the routes leading to God's heavenly kingdom reveals that Jesus validates three ways of expressing faith in himself. The faith of the intellect based on the Bible, the creeds and church dogma and doctrines. The faith of the emotions based on a statement of a personal relationship with Jesus following a conversion experience such as being born again. The faith of actions based on loving your neighbour as yourself as Jesus taught. This last aspect of belief in Jesus, expressed through living by his values based on the love of our neighbour, is equally valid, whether or not we also subscribe to a verbal expression of faith. The faith of actions brings Christians together. Doing good deeds through the love of our neighbour as advocated by Jesus is a route into heaven available to everyone Christian and non-Christian alike. All three separate expressions of faith provide us with a ticket to heaven. Thus when someone dies, we can gain great encouragement from recalling their acts of kindness and good deeds which will provide our loved one with a ticket to eternal life in heaven. A route which we are also on, as we also embrace those expressions of faith validated by Jesus, and are destined to meet with them in God's heavenly kingdom.

# 21 THE CHRISTIAN FAITH AND DEATH

The Christian faith opens our eyes to see death as a normal event which is to be welcomed and prepared for spiritually as well as practically. Christians have all had a foretaste of that resurrection life having been baptised into the death and the resurrection of Jesus. So they can look forward to death for the best is yet to come.

Our twenty-first-century society seeks to postpone and avoid death at all costs. Yet Paul, who is a Christian, just like any other Christian, in his New Testament writings, welcomes death. Writing in his Epistle to the Philippians (Phil 1:18b-26) Paul explains his view on life and death based on his experiences as a Christian. Paul's Christian view is that given a choice, he would rather die and be with Christ than stay alive. However, Paul chooses to stay alive solely to serve God and help others in their service of God, including those Christians at Philippi. Paul writes about living and dying; "I am hard pressed between the two: my desire is to depart and be with Christ, for that is far better; but to remain in the flesh is more necessary for you" (Phil 1:23,24). In writing this, Paul is not choosing something of which he is unaware. Paul already knows of the risen life with Jesus. Paul knows that the Christian faith enables him to experience that risen life with Christ. Paul knows that his resurrection life with Jesus is much better than this life in the flesh. Therefore, he can write that if given a free choice, he would now choose that resurrection life lived with Christ and be rid of this earthly life lived in the flesh.

We have come to regard Paul as a theological expert. Nevertheless, Paul does not write these things as a theological expert setting out difficult to understand doctrinal theories and concepts. Paul writes from the standpoint of his own experiences of being a Christian. Paul's experiences of the Christian faith are just the same as any other Christians' knowledge and understanding of the Christian faith. Paul is merely describing what every other Christian can also experience and know.

Paul explains how he is experiencing his risen life with Christ in his Epistle to the Romans (Rom 6:1-12). These are experiences common to all Christians. Paul is drawing attention to events which take place in the life of every Christian. Paul links these events to baptism because this makes it easier for him to explain what he wishes to teach us. Paul's teaching is easier to understand when explained within the symbolism of baptism. But in fact, as these events are an essential part of becoming a Christian. Then, for an adult, they must and do take place when a person becomes aware for the first time that they have become a Christian before they take the step of baptism.

Paul is speaking of adult baptism, which occurred after a person had already accepted the Christian faith. Baptism is the outward sign that a person has accepted the Christian faith. In Romans 6:1-12, Paul teaches us the following about how we can experience heaven in our earthly lives. Paul writes that Christians, through baptism, and therefore through becoming a Christian, have been baptised into Christ's death ("baptised into his death" (Rom 6:3). As a result of this they will also be raised to new life with him ("raised from the dead …….. to walk in newness of life" (Rom 6:4)). Therefore, Christians can experience being raised from death to new life with Jesus here and now. This experience and realisation occur the moment a person becomes a Christian. Paul teaches us that we must present ourselves to God as those who have been "bright from death to life (Rom 6:13). That is brought from death to life now in our earthly lives. The moment a person becomes a Christian, then they are united with Christ in his death to be immediately raised from death to new life with Jesus. Paul describes these events as happening at baptism to help people to understand his teaching by using the symbolism of baptism. Paul writes "Do you not know that all of us who have been baptised into Christ Jesus were baptised into his death? Therefore we have been buried with him by baptism into death, so that, just as Christ was raised from the dead by the glory of the Father, so we too might walk in newness of life" (Rom 6:3,4).

Walking in that newness of life takes place here and now in this life. Paul links the experience of becoming a Christian with both the experience of dying and being buried with Christ and the experience of being raised from that death and burial just as Christ was, to the new resurrection life. It is this new resurrection life that we now walk in. Paul has experienced all of this. He is explaining that this also should be the experience of all Christians. We walk "in newness of life now" in this life. Just as Christ died and was buried to the values of this world, so are we. We, like Jesus, are raised to the benefits of new life with Jesus. A newness of life which we walk in now. Paul is already experiencing that new resurrection life with Jesus. It was Paul's experience as a Christian. As the Christian faith is the same faith for all Christians, then what Paul has experienced will also be the experience of every other Christian. Paul also links this with the Christian experience of being dead to sin and no longer seeking to live by those values and desires which are sinful. Sin is the evil values and desires linked and rooted entirely to this earthly life. Following on from the death to sin, Christians have been raised to the new resurrection life, here and now. This new resurrection life is a life lived by the values of Jesus.

Paul writes, "Therefore, do not let sin exercise dominion in your mortal bodies, to make you obey their passions. ………………….but present yourselves to God as those who have been brought from death to life, and present your members to God as instruments of righteousness" (Rom 6:12,13). Paul teaches us that Christians are to present ourselves to God as those who have already been brought from death to life. In other words, Christians can experience that resurrection life here and now because we have already been brought from death to life. Further Christians become instruments of righteousness by living by God's values which are the values of God's heavenly kingdom. The heavenly kingdom where eternal life will be lived. In living by those values now then we are already living that eternal life in God's heavenly kingdom, where those values reign supreme. Paul knows this because he is already living by those values. Paul writes; "Do you not know that all of us who have been baptised into Christ Jesus were baptised into his death. Therefore, we have been buried with him by baptism into death, so that, just as Christ was raised from the dead by the glory of the Father, so we too might walk in newness of life" (Rom 6:3,4)]. Paul tells us that what he is experiencing is what all Christians should also experience. This newness of life which Paul is experiencing now, and which all Christians can experience now, is that eternal life lived with Jesus. At present, it is tangled up and caught up in this earthly life. Hence Paul longs to depart this earthly life to be with Christ unencumbered with his human life.

Paul is writing from his own experiences of being a Christian. Paul already knows what that resurrection life with Jesus is like so he knows what he is departing to when he writes "my desire is to depart and be with Christ" (Phil 1:24).

What Paul writes here should be very understandable to all Christians. For a Christian, resurrection is not only about "going to heaven when we die." It is also about experiencing that new resurrection life here and now through living by the values of God's heavenly kingdom here and now, just as Paul did. Paul is not a theologian explaining a theory. Paul is telling us his own practical experiences of life as a Christian. Paul describes this to his readers to confirm what they also are experiencing. Paul explains in his Epistle to the Romans how all Christians, just as he has, can also experience this new resurrection life here and now.

Paul writes in the context of Christian baptism because those first Christians had all been baptised as are Christians today. In Paul's time, the gospel was preached to adults. Adult Christians were baptised in response to their acceptance of the Christian faith. Unlike today where in our society, the vast majority of people are baptised as babies. The church administers baptism following the teaching of Jesus that Christians are to be baptised. This is set out in the commission of Jesus to his disciples at the end of Matthew's gospel (Mt 28:16-20) when Jesus tells his disciples to baptise all who accept the Christian faith. Paul explains that this acceptance of the Christian faith is symbolised and sealed by baptism. It involves a Christian's realisation that they have come so close to Christ, that they are one with Christ. Being at one with Christ, who is living his resurrection life now, means that Christians are in a position to share in Christ's resurrection life now. Paul explains this oneness with Christ by saying that Christian baptism symbolises that a Christian has been clothed in Christ (Gal 3:27). It is helpful to think of this as being disguised as someone by wearing their clothes. That someone is Christ. It is similar to a stage performance in which a skilled impersonator can disguise themselves in another's clothes. They then act so as to be mistaken for that other person on the stage. In like manner, Christians are to be imitators of Christ. They have to be so like Christ that they are mistaken for Christ. Paul writes; "As many of you who were baptised into Christ have clothed yourselves with Christ" (Gal 3:27).

On another occasion, Paul describes this "oneness" with Christ as "putting on the Lord Jesus Christ" (Rom 13:14) and in so doing shunning the values and desires of this world. In using the phrase "putting on the Lord Jesus Christ" Paul means that we put on, that is change into being Jesus. It is achieved through that closeness which we have with Jesus. Paul is explaining that this "oneness" with Christ means that Christians symbolically through baptism, but in fact at the moment when they became a Christian, have been baptised into his death and raised to new life with him. It means Christians have died to sin, that is the evil values and desires entirely linked and rooted to this earthly life and have been raised to the new life, here and now, living now by the values of Jesus (Rom 6:1-8). These values are also the values of God's heavenly kingdom. What Paul writes, he writes from his own experience. It is how Paul is experiencing his own Christian life. Also, this must have been how those first Christians living in Rome also experienced their own Christian lives. If their Christian experiences had been so different from those of Paul, they would have rejected what Paul was writing. They would have seen it as being meaningless and as not being in accordance with their own experience of being a Christian. The result would have been that they would have binned Paul's letter declaring that Paul had made a big mistake. If Paul's letters had not resonated with his fellow Christians, then they would not have been kept but would have been rejected and lost to us. This, those first Christians did not do. The fact that Paul's letters were preserved illustrates that the Christians of the first two centuries also agreed with Paul and felt this way about their faith.

Further, if what Paul was teaching had been outside of the experiences of his readers, then there was ample opportunity for this to be stated and used against him by Paul's enemies. We know that Paul had enemies, who were vehemently opposed to him and of whom he speaks about in his Epistles, for example, Gal 4:8-20; Phil 3:17-21. They would have seized on any aspects of Paul's teaching, which, did not resonate with his fellow Christians and condemned it as such. Thus, those first Christians must, like Paul, also have had a foretaste of that new resurrection life lived with Jesus. It is a foretaste, which all Christians begin to experience on becoming a Christian.

All Christians, can as Paul did, look forward to departing this earthly life to be with Christ. For like Paul, Christians know what it is like to live that resurrection life with Jesus. Thus, a Christian can welcome death as the gateway to continuing that resurrection life with Jesus in all its fullness unencumbered by our physical presence in this world. For a Christian death is the natural process necessary for a Christian to pass through to be raised to eternal life in God's heavenly kingdom. A life which Christians have already had a foretaste, as they already, here and now, live their lives by the values of God's heavenly kingdom. Thus Christians have every reason to look forward to dying. For the best is yet to come. Through displaying the faith of actions, non-Christians also demonstrate that faith in Jesus which will gain them eternal life. Jesus teaches, "I am the resurrection and the life. Those who believe in me even though they die will live, and everyone who lives and believes in me will never die." (Jn 11:25). Non-Christians, who have lived by the faith of actions, they too can look forward to dying for the best is yet to come.

# 22 THE CHRISTIAN FAITH AND HEALING

**Christian healing has a spiritual as well as a physical dimension. God's healing makes us whole spiritually but not always physically in answer to our prayers. It should temper our reactions should physical healing not occur.**

In the face of the Coronavirus, the Archbishops of Canterbury and York and other church leaders called for a day of prayer on 22nd March Mothering Sunday. President Trump called for a National Day of Prayer in America on 15th March. Each year America has a National Day of Prayer on the first Thursday in May.

History has seen almost 550 days of National prayer in England for God's help on the side of the nation in the face of plagues, wars and other National threats or to offer thanks for God's timely intervention. Seven such days were called during the last war. The most notable being one called for at the time of Dunkirk.

The first recorded National Day of Prayer is that of King Aethelred in the 10th century asking for God's help to defeat the coming Viking invasion. Praying for God's help to secure victory was the dominant theme of these days of prayer in the Medieval period as England was caught up in various wars and campaigns. They have been called for a variety of reasons. Some have been for Days of Prayer for Thanksgiving such as for the victory at the Battle of Waterloo 1815. In addition to wars and individual battles, Days of Prayer have been called for, for Royal events. These include prayers for the recovery from illness for monarchs, or for safe royal births and national thanks giving days for coronations and jubilees. National Days of Prayer have been called in the face of plagues (e.g. cholera epidemic of 1832) and famines (e.g.The Great Famine of Ireland 1845-52 a fast day was ordered on 24th March 1847). Monarchs and governments ordered these days. In the 20th century in an increasingly multicultural society, they had more and more been left to the Archbishop of Canterbury in collaboration with other religious leaders. Some days of prayer have failed for example the Battle of Yorktown in 1781 which was lost; Queen Caroline who died in 1821 despite the prayers of the nation for recovery. Failure was attributed not to the failure of prayer but to the fact that people had not prayed hard enough. The result often was that more prayers and more sincere praying and fasting was called for.

The reasons for such days was to ask God's help in events affecting the nation and to offer gratitude for his past help. So many took place because people felt that they did work. Plagues eventually died out (we now know) due to natural causes based on people's immunity and virus behaviour. Also, Britain was a powerful nation capable of winning wars. Thus, the National Days of Prayer did appear to be being answered by God. From 1500 to 1900, people believed that God had a plan for his world. When a nation strayed from that plan, God would send warnings for people to repent. These could be in the form of wars, famines, plagues or other disasters. To reform, the nation had to turn to God in prayer to ask for forgiveness for sins committed and pray for guidance once more to follow his will. Penance and fasts were also called for to assuage the sins of the nation and call off God's wrath. Thus, appeased God would return the nation to wealth and prosperity and peace and harmony. A simple view which was already being called into question. In the past, there were fierce debates as to whether a plague was God's punishment and warning or the result of natural causes. Other nations also have National Days of Prayer. In the past, two opposing countries could each be asking God's assistance to win the war in which they were fighting each other.

The Archbishops' call to prayer has not been asking God to spare the nation on the traditional lines outlined above. It has a different purpose. This call to prayer is to pray for healthcare workers and others fighting the Coronavirus disease, asking God's strength and guidance for them and thanking God for their work. To pray for the sick asking for their healing. To pray for people to love others by helping others, especially those in most need at this time.

The advent of the Coronavirus has come with a change in Christian thinking about praying. The pagan view of prayer in Biblical times was to use prayer to manipulate their gods to do them favours aided by the bribery of a gift of a sacrifice. The National Days of Prayer followed a similar pattern. The bribe, in this case, is that the nation would repent and once more follow God's ways. Our Christian prayers can sometimes follow the same pattern. Asking God for favours, in the form of protection from illness, healings or giving us worldly success, aided by the bribery of being a dutiful church member. Relying on individual sentences of scripture such as, "Ask, and it will be given to you:" (Mt 7:7). This is not a blank cheque, otherwise we would all be millionaires. The asking has to be within the will and purposes of God, which need first to be discerned. Of course, the supreme request that we can make is that we are allotted our place in God's heavenly kingdom. The advent of the Coronavirus has not resulted in the "ancient pagan like" prayers of a national wave of prayer asking God to spare the country or even to spare individual church congregations.

A time of prayer is primarily a deliberate setting aside of time and energy to become more aware of the presence of

First Aid in Bereavement

God with us. Then in the conscious presence of God, allowing time in quiet prayer to allow God's presence to infiltrate all our thoughts and plans. These prayers may be spoken out loud or prayed silently. Of course, this form of praying should be going on in our lives all of the time, whatever we are doing. There should be no need to make a special effort or time to do this. Times of prayer are, however, a stepping stone to achieving this.

From a Christian perspective, when someone dies, then issues linked to Christian faith and healing come to the fore. It is summed up by the question; "Why did not God heal the person in response to my prayers?" Such thoughts must be viewed in the context of our eternal relationship with God. Not just in the context of our temporal relationship with God. In the context of our eternal relationship with God. God, through Jesus, has prepared a place for us in his heavenly kingdom. It is the supreme good that can happen to us. Jesus tells us; "Do not let your hearts be troubled. Believe in God, believe also in me. In my Father's house, there are many dwelling places. If it were not so, would I have told you that I go to prepare a place for you? And if I go and prepare a place for you, I will come again and will take you to myself, so that where I am, there you may be also" (Jn 14:1-3). Christians, when faced with the situation where someone is suffering from a terminal illness, need to be aware that one of the outcomes which God has planned for is that this may be the occasion when Jesus will take that person to himself. A place where we can no longer physically interact with that person. Our prayers may be for a physical cure so that our physical interaction with that person can continue. But such a result, such a victory, is not the only result, not the only victory, God has in his store for us. That the person has died and is now in heaven with Jesus reveals God's victory just as assuredly as does a miracle cure.

In Biblical times the pagans view of the gods was very much temporal. They saw their relationship with their gods as being purely linked to this life. (Except for the gods of death and the afterlife.) They worshipped not one god but several gods, each with a specific role. Their interaction with each god was seen primarily in the context of trying to manipulate that god to do them favours in this life. Take, for example, Neptune who was the god of the sea. Before a sea voyage, a pagan would offer sacrifices to Neptune and prayers for a safe voyage. The thinking is that having given Neptune the present of the animal which had been sacrificed. Then in return, Neptune would do them a favour and grant them a safe passage. It was a sort of bribery. They sought to manipulate Neptune. Of course, when they had a pleasant sea voyage, they thought they had succeeded in influencing Neptune, and their faith in him and his powers increased. It worked to promote Neptunes standing for as the weather is good for sailing the majority of the time. Then the majority of sea voyages went off successfully. It conveyed the notion that their prayers and sacrifice had been successful and Neptune had revealed his power by ensuring a safe voyage.

As Christians, when we think of our relationship with God in purely temporal terms, we can be drawn into a similar way of thinking. We seek to manipulate God. We might, for instance, promise God that we will attend church every Sunday if he grants our prayers for healing. We might already be attending church with the hope that because we are doing this, God in return will protect our loved ones and us from such illnesses. Or worshipping God will persuade him to come to our aid with a miracle of healing should we or someone close be diagnosed as terminally ill. We are seeking to ingratiate ourselves with God and so be in a position to milk God for favours. Or we expect God to grant our wishes to keep us on board. It is not the relationship which God wishes to maintain. Though I am sure that God is accepting of whatever relationship we have with him. If it is one which could be improved upon, then there is always the opportunity to do that.

Praying to God for a miracle cure for someone suffering from a severe or terminal illness is what many people do automatically. This automatic response occurs should that person be a church attendee with a deep Christian faith or someone who attends church very infrequently, if at all. This response arises from a genuine concern that the terminally ill person be restored to their former good health. Thus having prayed to God in this way, should the patient die from the illness, it can have consequences for a person's belief in God. In considering this matter, we must remember that God is our loving heavenly Father. Just like an earthly father, God wants what is the very best for us. The supreme good which God wants everyone to have is eternal life. It is only finally achieved through our death and our resurrection to that eternal life.

In the event of prayers for healing not being answered then in the emotional heat of the moment, the Christian can respond with disappointment and even anger. In the case of a Christian or non-Christian anger at God can arise when it is felt that God has not answered our prayers for healing. In the case of a person with little or no faith, it may only confirm their view that there is no God. In the case of a deeply religious person, their anger can have an impact on their faith if their belief in a God of love who cares for them like a father is the bedrock of their faith. Their loss of a loved one, therefore, calls into question their faith in God's care and love, which up until now, they unquestioningly received from God. As a result of their prayers not leading to a miracle cure, they are left feeling very angry at God. It is because God has not fulfilled what they expected him to do from their understanding of and experience of God's love and care. They feel that because of his love for them, God should have cured the loved one through a miracle. Thus, preventing the loss of life and sparing the bereaved their grief. Such feelings of anger and disappointment can severely impact on a person's faith. The result on some occasions can be a complete loss of faith.

Traditionally when Christians pray for someone who is ill, especially if that illness is life-threatening, then the prayers are focused on a miracle cure. We pray that the person will be cured of their illness and made whole again. We deem our prayers to be answered when that person returns to their normal state of health which they were in before the illness. Thus, restored they can continue with their earthly life as before. This healing may take place not as a miracle cure but as a result of medical intervention. It is still often seen as God working his healing touch through modern medicine.

Should no healing take place and the person die, we can feel that our faith is being called into question. It can result in our anger at God for his seeming inactivity. This conclusion does not take account of the fact that the life for which God wishes to make us whole is that eternal life which God offers to all. We also need to remember that death is a natural end to everyone's earthly life. It is the portal through which we must all pass to continue, through our resurrection, in that eternal life which God gives to us. In this context, we also often do not take into account that all the people whom Jesus cured, including Lazarus, one day died. Thus, the ultimate good which Lazarus was to receive from God was his resurrection to eternal life for which his death would be the gateway. The restoring of earthly life to Lazarus was not the best event which was to happen to Lazarus. The best event was his resurrection to eternal life.

Many Christians, and for that matter, many other people, who would not claim a strong allegiance to the Christian faith, have come to see God's healing one-dimensionally. They see it as a solely physical healing, a miracle cure. It also has lead Christians and others not to fully understand the relationship between our lives in this world of time and space and our lives in God's heavenly kingdom. It stretches for eternity and is not limited by time and space. Lazarus though temporarily restored to this life in space and time, at a later date, had to pass through death to be raised to eternal life.

When Jesus speaks of the faith of the person involved or the faith of others, being responsible for healing someone, we must also acknowledge that spiritual healing, which also occurs. The wholeness arising from the healing is not limited to physical wholeness and the restoration of physical health. In the case of the people healed by Jesus, the realisation that their physical illness has been cured must have had a profound effect on their spiritual understanding of their relationship with God. There would have been spiritually the healing of any rift between themselves and God. It would have left them spiritually healed and spiritually whole in the sight of God. This feat of a person being made spiritually whole, in addition to having been cured of their physical illness by a miracle, is often overlooked. Jesus himself refers to it when performing some of his miracles. When healing the paralytic man brought to Jesus on a mat by his friends, Jesus says to him "Son, your sins are forgiven" (Mk 2:5). Revealing that the healing Jesus brings is not just visible physical healing.

In this miracle, we need first to consider that spiritual healing of the rift between that person and God. In this case, the rupture caused by sin. On the occasions when someone is physically cured through prayer, they are restored to physical wholeness. There will also be a restoration to spiritual wholeness when any breach with God is also healed.

In considering these issues, we must remember that God is our heavenly Father. Just like an earthly father, God wants what is best for us. The supreme good which God wants everyone to have is eternal life. It is only finally achieved through our death and our resurrection to that eternal life.

To be raised to eternal life, we must be spiritually whole to embark on that eternal life. Death is the normal and natural end of our earthly life for everyone, including Lazarus, and the precursor to continuing our life in God's eternal kingdom forever. As we pass through death, God makes us spiritually whole to embark on eternal life with him. In the final analysis, to achieve this spiritual wholeness, it is necessary to die. We can easily accept this of a 90 years old relative who dies after a full and vigorous life. As a result of our attachment to the pleasures of this life, we find it very difficult to accept this in the case of someone who dies young. Yet the 70 or 80 years of age difference is nothing when compared with the infinite number of years of eternal life.

Death is the normal and natural end of our earthly life for everyone and the precursor to continuing our life in God's eternal kingdom forever. As Paul explains in his First Letter to the Corinthians, our physical life will be replaced with a spiritual existence. It is only through death that our perishable bodies can be clothed with immortality as we are resurrected to that new life with God. We move from this perishable world of time and space to God's eternal, imperishable heavenly kingdom (1 C0or 15:42-46).

Thus, to focus solely on a physical cure, on physical wholeness, takes no account of the fact that we are in need of being made spiritually whole by God. As we pass through death, God makes us spiritually entire. By being spiritually complete, we mean being made whole from the damage inflicted on ourselves through living at odds with God's plan for our lives, through our sins. Our sins need God's forgiveness before we can be spiritually complete. It is what Jesus teaches us to pray for in the Lord's Prayer. (Forgive us our sins as we forgive those who sin against us). This damage is healed by God's mercy and his love for us. We should, therefore, be praying for the person to be made spiritually as well as physically whole by God. In so praying, we are helped to accept that death followed by resurrection is one of the ways through which God cures people. He does so by making them spiritually healed in readiness for eternal life with him. In the second letter of Peter (2 Pet 1:3-11), we read that Jesus Christ has the power to enable us to become "participants in the divine nature" (2 Pet 1:4). [The Eastern Orthodox Church draws on this verse to establish its teaching on Theosis or deification. Briefly, this teaching sets each human being the goal of leading a holy life through prayer, asceticism and deeds done, to restore God's image in themselves. The image in which everyone is created, but which has been damaged by the fall of Adam in the Garden of Eden. In doing this, they seek the assistance of God's grace. The result is that each individual can be deified, that is become like God as they were meant to be before the fall of Adam. They do not become Gods or merge with God but become participants of the divine nature. (The Protestant and Roman Catholic Churches see the fall of Adam as the origin of original sin.)]

God's healing seen only as a physical cure is too narrow a view of what God has in store for us. It fails to take into account the eternal nature of our lives and that heavenly home in God's eternal kingdom, which Jesus has gone ahead to prepare for us (Jn14:1-6). Jesus says to us; "Do not let your hearts be troubled. Believe in God, believe also in me. In my Father's house are many dwelling places. If it were not so, would I have told you that I go to prepare a place for you? And if I go and prepare a place for you, I will come again and will take you to myself, so that where I am, there you may be also" (Jn14:1-3).

This being so, the death of our loved one was that time for them when God made them spiritually whole, ready to take up forever their place in his kingdom. We can, therefore, entrust our loved one into God's safekeeping and be thankful to God for that, rather than angry with, God. For God, has miraculously made them spiritually whole, so that they can take their place with him in his heavenly kingdom. That is the greatest miracle God can perform, and he is prepared to do it for everyone. For the supreme good which God wants for everyone is to enjoy eternal life.

# 23 THE CHRISTIAN FAITH AND GRIEF'S BURDEN OF WORRIES

To encourage through explaining how the Christian faith can ease the burden of worry on the journey through grief.

The journey through grief can be described as a journey through worry. Having the Christian faith will not make these worries disappear as if by magic. The Christian faith is not a magic wand which will banish the burden of these worries which the death of a loved one will bring. A Christian, like everyone else, will have to face these issues, experience them and manage them. These worries are part and parcel of being a human being and are experienced by everyone. Christians are helped through this experience by following the teaching and example of Jesus. Also, by following his guidance, a Christian can set an example for others. Thus, revealing to others what is the best way to manage the worries which stem from a bereavement. Christianity helps us to manage our worries, both passively and actively.

These worries can be separated into concern arising from the many practical matters to be dealt with and worries stemming from our emotional response to the death of a loved one.

First of all, we will discuss issues relating to the worries which can arise from practical tasks which follow on from the death of a loved one. Many of these worries are similar too or an extension of the concerns we meet in our everyday lives. These worries begin at the very outset of our grieving and continue through it. They are revealed as we ask ourselves such questions as. Have I contacted the right undertaker? Is this a funeral service my loved one would want? Have I printed enough service leaflets? Have I contacted all the authorities I need to inform about the death? What should I do about my loved one's possessions? Should I move house? Additional worries arise in making these decisions; for now, they have to be made without the help and support of our loved one. Also, in grief, they can appear magnified because our grieving has sapped our energies and our will power. These are only a few examples of situations requiring practical decisions to be made with its accompanying worries, which are triggered following the death of a loved one.

Secondly, there are worries which arise as we seek to control the emotions which beset us on our journey through grief. They are revealed as we ask ourselves such questions as. Will this deep sadness ever go away? How will I cope? Will I ever get over this? What am I going to do with my life now? How will the children cope? How will I manage financially? Should I be doing this so soon after the death of my loved one? Worries arise about being ambushed by grief or being overwhelmed by our emotions which have been released as a result of the death of our loved one. These worries will be heightened when these emotions are so strong that they take over our lives as they sweep over us. It is particularly so in the case of feelings of panic, anxiety and fear, which for some can come at any time. Then there is the worry about how many times will I be yet again plunged into deep grief and despair in the days and weeks ahead. These feelings are aggravated by the fact that we no longer have our loved one for support and encouragement.

Jesus helps us to manage our worries arising from bereavement passively when he instructs us to cast our cares on him. As with all our concerns, whatever their source, Jesus provides us with a welcome relief so that we can relax and take stock of the situation facing us. We are instructed by Jesus to cast our worries on him for Jesus teaches us; "Come to me all you who are weary and are carrying heavy burdens and I will give you rest" (Mt11:28). This is to be no handing them over to Jesus and forgetting to do anything else about them. This is not the way of Jesus. We can pass over our burdens in prayer as we name each worry (out loud or silently) as we pass it over to Jesus. This is best done at night time. We can then enjoy a good nights sleep ready to once again pick up those worries in the morning when we are refreshed. Perhaps now with new ideas how to tackle them. Doing this brings welcome relief. This welcome relief is by nature passive, yet it is something we need to do at the beginning of our grieving and when necessary at many points throughout our grieving. It provides a welcome respite before we begin or continue the journey through grief. It is not a cure for or a means of preventing our worries, but it is a very welcome relief and easing of our burdens. It is not a passing of the buck to Jesus. It enables us to take stock and recharge our batteries ready for the next phase of our journey through grief.

Christianity also provides us with advice as to how to manage our worries arising from bereavement actively. We do this as we treat others with love and care and undertaking tasks as God would want them done. In doing this, we strive first and foremost for the kingdom of God and his righteousness (Mt 6:33). This pro-action will mitigate and alleviate our worries.

The focus on treating others with love and care arises from the teaching of Jesus to love our neighbours as ourselves. We need to respond to the needs of others, providing help and support and doing what is best for them. It includes our family and friends who are also affected by the death. It extends to acquaintances and those whom we meet as we fulfil the many practical tasks arising from bereavement. One immediate benefit of this approach lies in the breaking of the bonds that grief can trap us in. These bonds can envelop us should our lives become solely centred on ourselves and our grieving, to the exclusion of others. Loving and caring for others makes us look outward from ourselves and gives us a purpose in life. Further, as already explained elsewhere, helping others is the ideal antidote to grief. Doing these things with the focus on the love for and care of others enables a Christian to calm these worries and see them in their correct perspective.

Leading on from this, Jesus tells us that the proactive approach which we can take is to, "strive first for the kingdom of God and his righteousness" (Mt6:33). In other words, do things as God would want them done. This gives a focus and a purpose to our lives. It is especially so when dealing with the situations which give rise to our worries arising from bereavement. In Matthew's Gospel Jesus speaks about these and other worries when he says, "Therefore I tell you do not worry about your life" (Mt6:25). Jesus goes on to speak about the birds of the air neither sowing nor reaping nor gathering into barns; Jesus speaks of the lilies neither toiling nor spinning yet they beautifully adorn the fields (Mt6:25-34). Jesus tells us, like them, not to worry but to; "strive first for the kingdom of God and his righteousness" (Mt6:33).

Jesus is telling us not to worry. We can take worry out of our lives when we strive first and foremost for the kingdom of God and his righteousness, for they replace our worries as the focus of our lives. The two are linked for striving for God's righteousness will gain entry into the kingdom of God. Striving for God's justice means to do things by God's ways and in this way, get things done as God would want them done. It will help to calm our worries and provide our lives with a focus.

Our faith is that Jesus has gone ahead to prepare a place for us in God's heavenly kingdom and will also return to show us the way. Jesus tells us not to worry. In John's gospel, Jesus says; "Do not let your hearts be troubled. Believe in God, believe also in me. In my Father's house are many dwelling places. If it were not so, would I have told you that I go to prepare a place for you? And if I go and prepare a place for you, I will come again and will take you to myself, so that where I am, there you may be also" (Jn14:1-3). When looked at from this perspective, a Christian is striving for eternal life in all that they do. In the context of that eternal life, earthly worries are seen in their true light. Worldly burdens are confined to this period of time and space and have no eternal significance.

When we are striving for the kingdom of God, we are looking to gain eternal life in the kingdom of God. The decisions we make are made with this goal in mind. Our decisions will be based on loving and caring for and helping others and in this way, revealing our faith to the world. Doing everything with this as our motivation will dramatically reduce the impact of our worries.

The Christian faith will not take away the necessity of making those decisions which have the potential to cause us to worry. Those decisions will still have to be made. By positively making those decisions in the light of what we feel and know, God would want us to do as we strive for his righteousness and his kingdom. It takes away our need to fret or worry about the rights or wrongs of the decisions we have made. What is required of a Christian is to live out those decision-making situations as God wants us to. We do this by striving for the kingdom of God and his righteousness. God ensures that we can do this in every situation in life. Be it a good or bad situation, a joyful or sad situation or just an ordinary, mundane everyday situation. We have no cause to worry so long as we are striving to do everything for God. This means seeking to do what is right in his sight. Doing what we feel Jesus would do in those circumstances. We have every opportunity to do this in whatever situation or circumstance in life we find ourselves.

The Christian faith is not a magic formula or wand which will banish the burden of these worries which the death of a loved one will bring. A Christian, like everyone else, will have to face these issues, experience them and manage them. Christians are helped in doing this by following the teaching and example of Jesus as set out above.

Thus, it is by living out the Christian life by caring for others and seeking to do things as God would want them done that helps a Christian manage the worries which arise from bereavement.

# 24 THE CHRISTIAN FAITH AND THE EMOTIONS OF BEREAVEMENT

To explain how the Christian faith can ease the impact of the emotions felt on the journey through grief.

A Christian will face all of the emotional upheavals which bereavement brings. There is no magic formula which can take away the grief which follows the death of a loved one. Jesus wept when he heard of the death of Lazarus (Jn 11:35). God does not shield a Christian from the emotions arising from bereavement. As we shall see, God enables a Christian to manage these emotions through the working out of their Christian faith. God provides three different approaches for Christians to adopt as they seek to manage their grief through the three persons of the Trinity. For those who relate best to a father figure, we have God the Father to whom we can turn as a Father to lend us his strength and protection. For those who prefer a companion, brother or friend to accompany and support them, we have God the Son, Jesus, who will be with them always even to the end of time. For those who prefer more spiritual support, then we have God the Holy Spirit is our Helper, Comforter, and Advocate. The one who spiritually helps us cope with whatever befalls us in life. The Christian faith enables us to draw on God in one or all three of these forms to guide, comfort and support us on our journey through grief. Three different means of support to help us to manage our grief.

Also, the Christian faith prepares us for these emotions which arise from bereavement in three ways. The Christian faith enables us to control our emotions, to face death and to know where our loved one has gone.

First, in living out the Christian faith, a Christian will have already mastered the control of some of these emotions, for example, anger, in his everyday life, through his faith. Thus, a Christian is better able to face up to, deal with and control such emotions when they surface during bereavement.

Secondly, the Christian's faith enables a Christian to see death and face death as a normal and natural part of life, drawing our earthly life to a close. Christians are fully aware of this before the finger of death touches the life of someone close to them. In this context, a Christian sees death as God's plan for the end of our earthly life and the transition to the continuation of our eternal life in God's heavenly kingdom. Thus, being strengthened by their faith to face death as a natural part of life. The Christian is in a position to view the emotions experienced in mourning as a natural and healthy part of life and so not be caught unawares or off guard by them. This prevents these emotions from overwhelming a Christian and slipping out of their control. It mitigates their impact on the life of a Christian.

Thirdly a Christian knows that their loved one has gone to that place prepared by Jesus in our Father's heavenly kingdom (Jn14v1-3). This belief enables a Christian to see death in its true context, which is, as the gateway for us to continue to receive that greatest of good things, God's gift of eternal life in his eternal heavenly kingdom. The Christian, therefore, is in the best position to manage all of the emotions linked to grief should any begin to surface. As a result, these emotions are prevented from having an overwhelming or debilitating influence during a Christian's journey through grief.

The journey through grief involves the coming to terms with and the coping with the strong emotions which will sweep over us. A Christian can, as is the case with every-

# First Aid in Bereavement

one else, expect to experience these strong emotions. Jesus himself wept when he heard of the death of Lazarus (Jn11:35). For the reasons set out above the Christian faith does, however, enable these emotions to be seen in their proper perspective. It allows them to be managed in such a way that they do not control or unduly influence our lives. To this end, Jesus promises us that he will be with us throughout all our journeys, including our journey through grief, and he will never leave us. Jesus says, "I am with you always, to the end of the age" (Mt 28:20). This promise of Jesus is most clearly illustrated in the footprints prayer. It is a summary of the wonderful consolation which Jesus offers to all who turn to him.

The Footprints Prayer

I dreamt I was walking along the beach with the Lord, and
Across the sky, flashed scenes from my life.
For each scene I noticed two sets of footprints in the sand;
One belonged to me, and the other to the Lord.
When the last season of my life flashed before me,
I looked back at the footprints in the sand.
I noticed that many times along the path of my life,
There was only one set of footprints.
I also noticed that it happened at the very lowest
And saddest times of my life.
This really bothered me, and I questioned the Lord about it.
"Lord, you said that once I decided to follow you,
You would walk with me all the way;
But I have noticed that during the
Most troublesome times in my life,
There is only one set of footprints.
I don't understand why in times when I
needed you most, you should leave me".
The Lord replied, "My precious, precious
child. I love you, and I would never,

never leave you during your times of
trial and suffering.
When you saw only one set of footprints.
It was then that I carried you".
- Anon


There are many Bible passages which promise and reassure us that God will be with us come what may. As one example the older more traditional translations of Psalm 23 "The Lord's My Shepherd", used at funeral services, speak very poetically of this. The psalmist writes of God being with us as a shepherd is with his sheep at all times. The psalmist speaks of being in the valley of the shadow of death, yet fearing no evil for God is with him. He has God's rod and staff as a comfort (Ps23:4). In this word picture of God, God is seen as a shepherd. Just as a shepherd protects and cares for his sheep. Then God will do likewise for us with his rod and staff. In the middle-east shepherds carried both a rod, which is a thin stick and a staff, which was a club. This club was used to defend the sheep from wild animals and thieves. The rod served to extract the sheep when they got into difficult situations or to keep them close to the shepherd by applying gentle pressure on the flanks of the sheep. Thus, God is well prepared to keep us safe just as a shepherd is well prepared to keep his flock of sheep safe with his rod and staff. It is an example of God the Father, as a father, lending us his strength and protection, as mentioned above.

The words of Psalm 23 were written because the writer from his own experience knew them to be true. They were included in the Bible because people knew from their personal experience that these words were true. Since that time, countless millions of people have read those words in the Bible and have from their own experience found these words to be true. These words are true today. These words encapsulate God's promise to us that he will be a father to us, offering his strength and protection.

God does not say that he will shield us from and ensure that we have no knowledge or experience of the distress and suffering of death and grief. Instead, God says he will lend us his strength. He is protecting us as a shepherd protects his sheep in dangers and distressing situations, providing that protection and comfort in all circumstances. As a shepherd is with his sheep, so God is with us throughout our lives. He accompanies us all of the time, even in those final hours and minutes as our earthly life closes. God is with us as we wait at our loved one's bedside as they step into that eternal life which God has prepared for us. He is with us every step of the way on our journey through grief. He is with us every step of the way as we journey to and through our death.

Bereavement can be a very dark place, indeed. We have looked in detail in the chapter on 'Emotions and Bereavement', at the emotions which can affect our journey through grief. We will now see how a person's Christian faith enables them to manage and take control of these emotions.

On first hearing the news of the death of a loved one, there comes the denial which spawns the disbelief that the death of a loved one has occurred. There are the numbness and shock which inhibits us from coming to terms with the death of a loved one. Then we feel we are disorientated and struggle to grasp the reality of life and what is going on around us. There is the overwhelming sadness which the loss of a loved one can bring, which makes us feel that we are no longer in control of ourselves or our emotions. These feelings of sadness can be so great that we feel isolated, frightened and desolate. We suffer from the misery which will not go away. The Christian knows the calming presence of Jesus with them as a brother and a friend which they have also experienced at many other less traumatic times in their lives. This is an example of how God the Son, Jesus, is with us as a friend to turn to even to the end of time (Mt 28:20). The Christian, as on those passed occasions, is again able to call on that calming presence of Jesus. The calming presence of Jesus ensures that we see all of this in the context of eternity. Our faith informs us that our loved one is not lost but has just gone on before. Where they have gone, we too will follow one day, to that place where Jesus has gone to prepare a place for us. Jesus tells us; "Do not let your hearts be troubled. Believe in God, believe also in me. In my Father's house are many dwelling places. If it were not so, would I have told you that I go to prepare a place for you? And if I go and prepare a place for you, I will come again and will take you to myself, so that where I am, there you may be also" (Jn14v1-3). It is a reassurance that Jesus has anticipated our deaths, and there is a place prepared for us. This knowledge ensures that a Christian is not shocked or overwhelmed with sadness. These events are part of life. Death is a natural part of life and is just a stepping stone to our continued existence in God's eternal kingdom. Christians, therefore, do not need to fear death. They do not need to deny it or to be numbed by it. Instead, they can accept, at face value, the news that someone has died. Christians know death to be a natural part of life. As such, death will happen, so we have no need or inclination to deny or disbelieve that death has occurred. A Christian can, therefore, begin their journey through grief without the delays due to disbelief and denial. Confident that Jesus, the one who has conquered death, will be their constant companion and guardian. Yes, for the Christian, there will still be quiet times of sadness. But, there will not be an overwhelming sadness or a sadness which leaves them fearful because of its intensity. It will be a sadness which enables a Christian to understand the sorrow of others and help them on their similar journeys. For if Christians are to help others, then they must understand the situation from having been there themselves.

The disorganisation and confusion which follows the death of a loved one are also present in a Christian. There are many practical tasks to be done, and it is hard to focus our minds for any length of time to do them or in fact, to build-up the enthusiasm to do them. However, for Christians, knowing the presence of Jesus with them, this gives them calmness and a goal. A goal to do these things for the benefit of others as Jesus would wish them to be done. It includes the recipients of all the necessary paperwork and administration generated when someone dies. Doing these tasks for Jesus as he would want them to be done gives us a goal for doing them and makes them much less burdensome.

A Christian also still feels the yearning for the presence, the touch and the reassurance brought by the loved one who has died. Christians will use up energy searching in their memories for the loved one as they yearn to have them back. However, the sharp edge of this yearning will be blunted by the knowledge that God's promises will be honoured. A Christian knows that the place where the loved one has gone is the place prepared by Jesus in his father's house (Jn14v1-3). The Christian's searching is curtailed for the Christian knows where their loved one is to be found. They have been relocated to their Father's house, which is heaven.

The Christian is not immune from the feelings of anxiety, panic and sometimes fear. These arise when the mourner realises that they are now alone bereft of the company, comfort, help and advice of their loved one. The Christian becomes aware of the new roles they have to fulfil, which were once the preserve of the deceased. These roles might include that of now being a single parent, or of having to deal with finances and financial problems or of now having to do the domestic chores. There are a great variety of new circumstances to cope with, now alone with no support or advice from the deceased partner. There will also be a fear of what the new and very different future may hold. In such a situation, a Christian can turn to his task of serving Jesus and doing what Jesus wants him to do. This will involve serving other people and doing what is of benefit to them. It is summed up by the command of Jesus to love our neighbour as ourselves. Christians willingly undertake their new roles in their new circumstances. They know that in doing them, then Jesus is being served through the serving of other people. It brings stability and purpose to a Christian' life. This is also enhanced by the knowledge that Jesus is with them at all times.

Fear and anxiety will also arise as the death of the loved one is a reminder of a Christian's mortality. Here again, faith firmly based on God's promises is a comfort. A Christian can face death in the sure knowledge that Jesus has defeated death and that his victory is a victory for all. Death holds no fear, for a Christian knows that Jesus has gone before to prepare a place for them in his Father's and their Father's house, which is heaven.

The word grieve gives us the word grievous, which means bringing about physical suffering as in the case of the crime of GBH, grievous bodily harm. Grieving has a tangible impact upon us from sapping our energy and leaving us tired and exhausted, to physical symptoms of dizziness, headaches, heart palpitations and suppressing the immune system making colds and flu and other illnesses more likely. The calming influence of the Christian faith, knowing that our lives are safe in the hands of our heavenly Father who is God, enables a Christian to escape the worst influences of these physical symptoms because a Christian's confidence is placed in a God who is their comfort and help. It removes that stress which is generated by uncertainty and fear, which can trigger those physical symptoms and suppress the immune system.

The death of a loved one can precipitate an emotional outburst. An event or a word may trigger it. It may arise following the build-up of stress and tension. These emotional outbursts, which at times can seem to be taking over our minds, can have their root in anger, terror, resentment, blazing rage, regret and hate. A Christian with their faith firmly based on the understanding that Jesus is with them at all times and that they are walking with Jesus will have such outbursts well under control in their ordinary lives. A Christian is well aware that such uncontrolled outbursts are contrary to the will of Jesus. Their uncontrolled surfacing following the death of a loved one will be less likely in a Christian. Christians already know how to control such emotions and reject such outbursts, for they are contrary to following in the footsteps of Jesus. Such eruptions, not being part of the Christian's make-up, is the best way of ensuring that bereavement will not trigger such outbursts. Should any of these emotions arise, then, the Christian knowing that Jesus is a constant companion, would want to rein them in, following the wishes of Jesus and within the strength of Jesus. In this way, the faith of the Christian is ideally placed to counter such emotional outbursts, particularly that of anger.

Anger can also arise from feeling that the death is not fair or deserved. Or anger can be directed at medical staff or carers or oneself or God or the deceased loved one. Such outbursts of wrath are already constrained by the Christian's belief that uncontrolled anger is not the way of Jesus. A Christian's belief that though we do not fully understand God's ways, we can trust God to be working things out for our good, helps the Christian to control and calm such anger and frustrations.

Further, a Christian has the belief that when we die, we go to that place prepared for us in heaven by Jesus, and this is the supreme good that can happen to us. This belief enables a Christian to see the death of a loved one in this context. The notions of fairness or what we deserve pale into insignificance, against that highest good of all, that our loved one has gained their place in heaven, which itself is undeserved. The Christian knows that this is undeserved, for it is achieved through the intervention of Jesus, by his death for us and through the undeserved grace, love and mercy of God.

To blame others for their loss, the surgeon, the carers or even the deceased for departing and leaving them is not naturally a part of a Christian's make-up. For the Christian would seek first to see the good in others and not the blame in them. All of this is following a Christian's faith to love our neighbour (Mk 12:31) as well as our enemy and those who persecute us (Mt 5:43,44). Thus, unjustified anger at others is not part of the Christian faith or in a Christian's make-up. The Christian is well placed to control such feelings should they begin to emerge.

Turning to justifiable anger at mistakes or malpractices which had a part in the resulting death. Then the Christian, concerned in establishing on earth that justice which exists in God's heavenly kingdom, is well placed to pursue the legitimate righting of these wrongs, by reporting them to the appropriate authorities.

Rage, resentment and hate are similarly not part of the Christians make-up as they seek to walk with Jesus. Therefore, a Christian is well placed to control and defuse such feelings. A Christian has already learnt to recognise the undesirability of these emotions and thus, how to control and minimise their effect through his Christian walk with Jesus.

The feelings of guilt which can accompany the death of a loved one are also emotions for which the faith of the Christian acts as an antidote. A Christian may well acknowledge such thoughts and feelings passing through their mind, but through their faith, they know that there is no foundation for any of these feelings of guilt. It is in such situations that a Christian can draw on the help of God the Holy Spirit, who is our Helper, Comforter, and Advocate. The Holy Spirit provides spiritual support and is a comforter to our souls should they be tortured by guilt. The Holy Spirit reassures us of God's forgiveness. It allows a Christian to understand that they need not feel guilty before God for any of these things. A Christian is empowered to see things in a different light as a result of their Christian faith.

There is the guilt in the form of survival guilt when someone feels guilty of having survived when others have died. A Christian will see the fact that they are still alive as a further opportunity to continue to serve God in this life, which will outweigh any feelings of survival guilt.

Enjoyment guilt occurs when, after the death of a loved one, someone feels sincere regret that they are experiencing enjoyment. They think that they are somehow letting down the deceased loved one. Concerning enjoyment guilt, a Christian lives life in the love of God and seeks to love other people. This love would encompass the desire that should they have predeceased their loved one. They would have wanted their loved one to be happy in their continuing earthly life. Similarly, a Christian knows that their deceased loved one would also wish for them to have happiness in their remaining years of life. Thus, enjoyment guilt would have no part in the life of a bereaved Christian.

Relief guilt occurs when a person feels relief and even thankfulness that their loved one has died. It can arise as a result of the relief that the loved one is now no longer suffering. It can occur as a result of feelings of relief that the mourner is no longer called on to spend time and energy caring for or visiting the dying loved one. This feeling of guilt can also arise because of the wish that the suffering is over for the patient. This wish is seen as somehow having contributed to or hastened the death, or let down or is seen as being disloyal to the deceased.

Concerning relief guilt, a Christian fully realises and accepts that death is a part of life marking the ending of this earthly life. That ending will be brought about by a particular illness, the cause of death on the death certificate. Should any suffering be caused by that fatal illness, then the pain is a part of and solely results from that illness. Christians will thus see death as the natural means of release from that suffering. Concerning relief felt that the mourner no longer has to give of their time and energy to care for or visit the loved one. Christians will undertake these tasks out of love and see them as part of their Christian witness. There is, therefore, no need for guilt to be felt, even if the feelings of relief that the death has occurred do arise. Thus, the Christian will be spared the further anguish of relief guilt.

Also, over and above these considerations, should any of these feelings of guilt arise, then, this guilt can be assuaged as the Christian turns to God for forgiveness. Christians know that through God's grace, they will receive that forgiveness.

Christians, who seek to love and serve others, are unlikely to have feelings of regret for not calling an ambulance

# First Aid in Bereavement

sooner or insisting that someone sees their doctor earlier. This is because the whole of a Christian's life is lived in the service of others and doing what is best for others. Having done their best for the deceased, then there is no place for regret in the life of a Christian. Should such emotions begin to surface later, the Christian is in a position to view them in their correct context. If necessary, to seek and receive God's forgiveness and so disarm these emotions rather than to dwell on them with debilitating consequences.

A Christian just like everyone else who has been bereaved, has a mind full of the memories of their lost loved one. A chance incident may unexpectedly trigger these, or a Christian may choose to recall them as they look for example, at old photographs. Memories are a gift from God. They enable the reliving and the recalling of happy times from the past. In much the same way as we would choose to recall those happy memories when our loved one was here to reflect on them with us. Through recalling those memories, a Christian can relive these times and feel once again the enjoyment they first brought. They enable the happy times spent with their loved one to be appreciated and reflected on once again. Christians will also have feelings of sadness, emptiness and regret which such memories can bring These feelings will be mitigated by feelings of happiness, nostalgia, thankfulness and gratitude for the memories of their life with their loved one. These thanks will from time to time be expressed to God by a Christian openly in prayer. This thankfulness is directed to God, the provider of this world and therefore, the source and provider of those happy times spent with the loved one. Memories experienced in this spirit of thankfulness to God enable the Christian to experience these memories with feelings of nostalgia, warm appreciation and joy. It avoids being plunged into deep grief which the recall of such memories can trigger.

As people journey through grief, their lives become changed, as they build a new life without the physical presence of their loved one. The Christian faith is an aid to effecting these changes. A Christian serves others as he seeks to live his life in the service of God. Thus, Christians can adapt to the life-changing event of the death of a loved one as they continue to live their lives seeking the same goal of serving God and other people. The faith of a Christian will enable them to continue doing the will of God in the changed circumstances following the death of a loved one. In just the same way as they did when their loved one was alive.

A Christian is not freed from the emotions which affect everyone on their journey through grief. Instead of God sparing a Christian from these emotions. God, provides the means for a Christian to understand and manage the full range of emotions which are to be met on their journey through grief through the faith which a Christian has. This then enables a Christian to serve God better and help others who are also on their journey through grief, as a result of experiencing at first hand that journey through grief.

God does not, nor does he claim to, ensure that a Christian will never experience the loss of a loved one or the attendant emotions and events, which inevitably follow on from that loss. The fact that Christians experience the emotions which everyone else does on their journey through grief makes perfect sense. For a Christian must experience life in precisely the same way as everyone else to be a guide and helper to others, for this was how Jesus lived. He was not immune to the emotional and social tribulations of life in his times. Jesus wept when he heard of the death of his friend Lazarus (Jn 11:35). Jesus did not receive God's protection and shielding from suffering, death and grief. As a result, Jesus has shown us the way to manage these issues in life. Jesus has shown us that he knows how to deal with every issue arising in life and death. God shows us that to cope with such situations, we must follow in the footsteps of Jesus. God shows us that, just as he was with Jesus in these situations, so also, he will be with us.

Those who see God as some sort of Dutch uncle beyond the clouds may well have the delusion that God should shield and protect his followers and their loved ones from death. In so doing, God will also protect them from the grief which follows the death of a loved one. Some Christians are so convinced that this should be God's role that when the death of a loved one occurs with its ensuing grief, the natural consequence of the death of a loved one. Then they reject God because, in their eyes, God has failed to protect them from the tragedy of the death and the resulting deep sadness of grief. So much so, that these events may result in them abandoning their faith altogether. In such cases, their faith has been built on sand as Jesus describes in the Parable of the House built on Rock (Mt 7:24-27; Lk 6:47-49). Such people need to revisit their faith and rebuild it on the rock of Jesus. Then they will discover that God does protect them from death through his provision of eternal life.

Just as Jesus had to experience the grief and sorrows of this life, including his death on the cross, so that he could be our companion, helper and saviour. Then so also must Christians experience grief, just as other people do, if a Christian is to be a help, guide and comfort to others. It is only after experiencing these things that a Christian can hope to understand how to be of help to others. Otherwise, a Christian could be no help because they have no awareness or understanding of what other people are feeling, suffering or experiencing.

God wants us to stay positive about what is happening to us in our lives. A Christian's faith in God enables them to do this. Throughout his ministry, Jesus was positive. He saw everything in the light of fulfilling God's will. All that he did was done with the quiet confidence and calm of knowing he was accomplishing that ultimate of positives, doing the will of God. Faith is not a blind trust. It is based on our real-life experiences. Our real-life experiences that there is a God who loves and cares for us. When we emerge from the valley of the shadow of death, that period in our lives of grief and mourning, then looking back we can see that it was God and our faith in him which sustained us. It is just one of the real-life experiences which enable a Christian to know that to have faith in God is a sure foundation. It permits a Christian to stay positive through life's ups and downs even when we travel through the valley of the shadow of death.

Should we have just lost a loved one and we meet with someone else who has also experienced bereavement. We need no introduction for after exchanging a few words we realise that the two of us are on the same wavelength. We are in somebody's company with whom we can share our deepest thoughts and concerns relating to our shared experiences on our separate journeys through grief. It is because we know we are in the company of someone who has endured the self-same experiences which we have.

It is a similar experience when, as Christians, we recognise the presence of Jesus with us. We realise that we are in the presence of someone who has experienced life with all its ups and downs. Jesus lived this earthly life and experienced the self-same experiences which everyone has experienced. Some of those experiences occurred at his death on the cross and which we know that we will never have to experience. Jesus knew tears and laughter. Jesus knew times of celebration and times of sorrow. Jesus knew times of acclamation and times of condemnation. Jesus knew birth and death, the horrible, cruel death of a person rejected, reviled, and condemned to die alone on a cross. Jesus was at the wedding in Cana (Jn2v1-12) and the graveside of Lazarus (Jn11v1-44). Jesus rode into Jerusalem in triumph on the first Palm Sunday (Mk11v1- 10) and walked out of Jerusalem carrying his cross in condemnation (Mk15v16-27). Jesus was born in a stable (Mt1v18-25) and died on the cross (Mk15v42-47). When we meet with Jesus through faith, we likewise know we are in the presence of someone who is on the same wavelength as ourselves. It is so because Jesus has experienced all that it is to be a human being.

The Christian faith is well able to guide us on the journey through grief. The Christian faith informs us that God is with us in all we do even as we walk in the valley of the shadow of death. God is there to comfort and guide us for his rod and staff, are our comfort (Ps23v1-5). We have the promise of Jesus that he will be with as forever; "I am with you always to the end of the age" (Mt28v20). Jesus also tells us; "I will ask the Father, and he will give you another Advocate, to be with you forever. It is the Spirit of Truth" (Jn14v16,17). It, of course, refers to the gift of the Holy Spirit. The Greek word, which is translated 'advocate' in the NVRS Bible, can also be translated Comforter or Helper. Some translations of the Bible do use these words. In times of distress and grief, a comforter or helper is sorely needed. On these occasions, the Holy Spirit is our Comforter and Helper.

It is another example of the genius of God. For this is the way, God provides all the comfort and help which we might want through the three persons of the Trinity. As we have already seen for those of us, who relate to a father figure, we have God the Father who guides and comforts us even though we walk in the valley of the shadow of death. For those of us who prefer a companion or brother or friend to accompany and guide us, we have Jesus who will be with us always even to the end of time. For those of us who prefer more spiritual support, we have the Holy Spirit, our Helper, Comforter, and Advocate. The one who helps us cope with whatever befalls us in life. The Christian faith enables us to draw on God in one or all three of these forms to guide, comfort and support us on our journey through grief. We are thus enabled to manage the emotions which bereavement brings with it. God does not promise to spare us from the emotions associated with grief. But God does promise to be our companion and guide on our journey through grief enabling us to continue our life in his service.

# 25 CONCLUSION

It cannot be stressed enough that each person's experience of grief will be individual to themselves. We grieve because we have loved. The depth of our grief is a measure of the depth of our love. Each person has to come to terms with their grief in their way. The most important factors which influence the impact of grief are the closeness of the relationship, the length of the relationship and the previous experiences of bereavement. Of these, the closeness of the relationship is by far the most significant. A close spouse or partner relationship may leave the survivor still deeply grieving a decade and more after the death. The feeling of loss may be such that heartache may even be being triggered by seeing two people walking hand in hand. Though this may mainly be inward grieving for the survivor will in all probability by this length of time have learnt how to hide grief by "putting a brave face on it." Such can be the lasting power of the grief spawned by a bereavement.

As has been seen, the Christian faith does not shield a person from grief. Christians, have to come to terms with their grief through the Christian faith, which can significantly assist them in doing this.

I have purposefully not referred to any personal experiences of grief. They can be found movingly described in many of the books written on this subject. These books, together with others on the topics of bereavement, death and grief, can be found on websites such as Amazon books. Their titles reveal the nature of their contents. Instead, I have focused on those aspects of grief which are experienced by all. It has been done to reinforce that grief is and always has been a common emotion shared by everybody. It has broadly the same effect on everyone. Therefore, people should feel free to talk about this collective experience and in so doing mutually ease their pain with their own first aid. It is hoped that this book will give people the confidence to do so. In the sensitive area of grief and bereavement relating to children, which is not covered in this book, the following books are very helpful; Separations Death by Janine Amos; Mamas Going to Heaven Soon by Kathe Martin Copeland; Children and Bereavement by Wendy Duffy; Michael Rosen's Sad Book by Martin Rosen; Badgers Parting Gift by Susan Varley.

Death is the conclusion to life on earth. Growing numbers of people see it with more finality as the conclusion to existence full stop. Many more see death not as a full stop but as a question mark. The closing chapters of this book should have helped people to know the answer to that question (mark) is the one given by Jesus. To the question, "What happens when we die?" Jesus replies, "You have eternal life." Jesus teaches that those who have faith in him will not perish but have life eternal. Jesus also shows that this faith in him has three expressions. These are the faith of the intellect, the faith of the emotions and the faith of actions. The faith of the intellect and the faith of the emotions are to be predominantly found in churches and chapels. However, the faith of actions is revealed when people follow Jesus by loving their neighbour as themselves. This solidarity with Jesus can be found everywhere, in Christians and non-Christians. Jesus does not require those who minister to the needy to do it in his name. He requires them to do it. If you find that hard to believe, read the words and deeds of Jesus in the gospels for yourself. Read them with one question in your mind, "What does this teach me about eternal life?" (This is explained in my book "Tickets to Heaven.")

People are to respond to Jesus by putting their faith in him. In the gospels, Jesus tells us that through faith in him, we will gain eternal life. Jesus says, "For God so loved the world that he gave his only Son, so that everyone who believes in him may not perish but may have eternal life" (Jn 3:16). Jesus does not define this faith in the form of dogma or creed. What Jesus does do is to set out the many routes by which we can travel to God's heavenly kingdom and there enjoy that eternal life. By looking at the routes, Jesus sets down, which lead to God's heavenly kingdom; we can see that Jesus validates these three ways of expressing faith in him. Each expression can stand alone or be interwoven with the others.

As we stand at the graveside of our loved one. We will be able to reflect how, over the years, they have experienced times of celebration and happiness and times of tragedy and sadness. You will be able to recall those times which you shared with them. I wonder how many people your loved one met over those years? I wonder how many times they influenced for good the people whom they met? You will be able to recall the times that they motivated you for good. That is all that God asks of us that we influence others for good. I wonder how many people you have met in your lifetime? We do not know the answers to such questions. Only God knows those answers. For Jesus tells us in Luke's gospel "Are not five sparrows sold for two pennies? Yet not one of them is forgotten by God. Indeed the very hairs of your head are numbered. Don't be afraid;*(Jesus tells us for in God's eyes)* you are worth more than many sparrows." (Lk12:6,7). (The words in italics are mine.)

Jesus also tells us "In my Father's house are many rooms; if it were not so, I would have told you. I am going to prepare a place for you."(Jn14:2) We remind ourselves when we say the Lord's Prayer that God is our heavenly Father. So, it is with confidence that we commit our loved one into Gods safekeeping as we come to reflect on and celebrate their life with us. We still have our journey through grief to undertake, but its pain is much more tolerable when we know the new location of our loved one. It is in God's heavenly kingdom.

For those who see death not as a question mark but as a full stop. The end of all existence. This book can still be of benefit. It provides a route map through grief. Life's worst stresses and strains come when we are in unknown territory. Or feel events are out of our control. Or when there is seemingly no end in sight to our struggles. This book provides a route map of the journey through grief. It ensures that a person can know where they are on their journey as well as being able to see how close they are to the journey's end. The mourner is also aware that their journey through grief is a natural event in life which everyone will experience at some time in their lives. This knowledge enables them to discuss their grief with others in a similar position, knowing that what they are experiencing is normal. Such discussions are a way of administering first aid to our pain. All of this reduces the stress of bereavement. The mourner can see their location on the map of grief and chart their movement to its end.

Though bereavement brings with it pain and sorrow, Jesus reassures us that God created us for eternal life with him. Faith in Jesus will accomplish this. A faith which can be practical and applies to all people who care for others, the faith of actions, as well as a verbal faith, the faith of the intellect or the emotions. It should hearten our grieving with the knowledge that one day we shall all meet again in God's nearer presence.

Printed in Great Britain
by Amazon